Starting out with
Native Plants

Starting out with
Native Plants

Charlotte de la Bédoyère

New Holland

First published in 2007 by
New Holland Publishers (UK) Ltd
London · Cape Town · Sydney · Auckland
Garfield House, 86–88 Edgware Road
London W2 2EA
United Kingdom
www.newhollandpublishers.com

80 McKenzie Street
Cape Town 8001, South Africa

Level 1, Unit 4, 14 Aquatic Drive
Frenchs Forest, NSW 2086, Australia

218 Lake Road, Northcote
Auckland, New Zealand

ISBN 978 1 84537 669 7

Senior Editor: Clare Sayer
Production: Hazel Kirkman
Design: Andrew Barron/Thextension
Editorial Direction: Rosemary Wilkinson

10 9 8 7 6 5 4 3 2 1

Reproduction by Modern Age Repro,
Hong Kong
Printed and bound by Times Offset,
Malaysia

Contents

Introduction

To see a World in a Grain of Sand
And a Heaven in a Wild Flower,
Hold Infinity in the palm of your hand
And Eternity in an hour.

THESE HAUNTINGLY EVOCATIVE LINES BY
William Blake epitomise all that is wonderful in
the natural world. When it was written some two
centuries ago, he undoubtedly would have
considered flowers growing in the wild as native:
there was as yet no debate about what was native
and what was not. Plants had been brought to
Britain from all over the world for centuries, but it
was the Victorians who popularized the cultivation
of them in gardens, and who found these aliens
irresistible. Some of these exotics escaped into the
wild, and some (the most infamous is probably the
Rhododendron), suddenly faced with much more
auspicious conditions than in their birthplace,
became rampant and destructive. This, coupled
with the Industrial Revolution and population
explosions resulted in the gradual taking over of
wild places – something that accelerated out of all
proportion in the twentieth century.

The result is that, two hundred years later,
millions of pounds are being spent in endeavours
to eradicate some of these foreign species in order
to restore habitats for the original flora and fauna,
and to guard the ever-dwindling remaining ones.
This has sparked off many debates, regarding what
really are indigenous plants and animals.

What is a native plant?
Frankly, I do not think anyone really knows for
certain. There are many that fall into grey areas. I,
and I think others, had always assumed that what
were present on these islands when they broke away
from mainland Europe about six thousand years ago
constituted as good a criterion as any. This seems no
longer true. Modern technology such as carbon
dating and DNA testing has made it possible to
unearth and discover all kinds of new facts that are
causing endless confusion. Many botanical names
have changed – not very popular among
horticulturists and amateurs such as myself. All our
reference books continually become out of date!

In addition, with so many purists around,
the debate has become rather more esoteric and
academic, and seems to be looking backward
rather than forward. For instance, a plant with all
the right qualifications that has managed to break
out of its original habitat, whether by human
intervention, birds, wind or some other means, is
classified as 'alien' according to *The New Atlas
of the British and Irish Flora* (Oxford University
Press). One can understand the reasoning, but it
does not seem to allow for natural evolution,
especially in these years of climate change. It also
means that if a native plant grows in your garden,
regardless of whether you put it there or not, it
would not be considered native. Obviously plants
have chosen certain habitats as being best suited to
them, but, personally, I think it matters little
where a plant with all the right credentials grows
and thrives.

Why grow native plants?
Although there are many garden plants that are
good for wildlife, I think all conservationists agree
that collectively native species are the ones that
sustain the greatest biodiversity. After all, these
plants have simultaneously 'grown up' for centuries
with all the other wildlife, and are now best suited
for each other. This applies to the top mammals
(those that are extant) such as deer and badgers,
and also to birds, down to the tiniest insect, and not
least to the countless creatures living in the soil that
are invisible to the naked eye.

Also, by growing as many native species as
possible, you will be recreating, in a small way,
habitats that sustain wildlife. These natural places
have dwindled to horrendous and alarmingly low
proportions. At present only about 1 to 2 per cent
of ancient woodlands remain, as do only about 3 per
cent of grassland meadows, and other habitats have
shrunk to equally pathetic percentages.

But, you will surely ask, what difference can my
small garden possibly make? The answer is: a great
deal. Reports and surveys show that gardens are
becoming increasingly important for plants and
wildlife. According to the British Trust for
Ornithology, some species of bird have not only
halted their decline but are on the increase – all due
to domestic gardens.

Naturally, most people tend to empathize best
with birds, butterflies (moths are woefully

neglected) and other beautiful or 'cuddly'-looking animals – the hedgehog being one of them. But we should really embrace all of nature's creatures, including spiders, beetles and seemingly noxious insects – they are all part of nature's wonderfully interdependent biodiversity.

There are many other reasons why gardens are becoming increasingly important to wildlife. Exact figures are difficult to come by, but there are an estimated 15 million gardens in the UK covering some 270,000 hectares. This is about 3 per cent of all the land in the UK and is greater than all the nature reserves and about double the area of ancient woodland still in existence!

A sponsored survey was carried out in Sheffield by BUGS (Biodiversity in Urban Gardens in Sheffield) in order to assess what resources urban gardens provided for wildlife. The gardens were randomly selected with no particular leanings one way or the other. This analysis produced some extraordinary facts. If the resultant figures from the sampled gardens were scaled up to the whole of the city, they showed that Sheffield would have more than 25,000 ponds, 45,000 nest boxes, nearly 60,000 compost heaps, and 360,000 trees. The population of Sheffield is 513,000. It was also found that nearly one-third of our native species grow there.

As far as I know, no one knows how many gardens have either partially or wholly been turned over to indigenous flora and fauna, but numbers are certainly increasing as more and more people become aware of the plight of wildlife. Just imagine the effect if even a relatively small percentage of all the 15 million gardens became wholly or even partially wildlife-friendly!

Finally, there is another very good reason why you should grow true native species: by doing so you may well be building up a valuable genetic reservoir of plants that appear to be depleting daily in the wild.

About this book

First of all, I do not much like the word native, or alien for that matter, so as far as the rest of this book is concerned I will largely, like Blake, use the terms 'wild' when referring to native species.

The first part concentrates on acquiring wild seeds and/or plants and on how to grow them. Originally, I told the publishers I would not include orchids, since their cultivation was very specialised and difficult. I take it all back! In just a few years enormous strides have been made and a great deal more is now known about growing these fascinating and beautiful plants. A short section on orchids is therefore included. There follows a section on different meadows, which, if put together, are home to nearly all our wild plants.

The largest section consists of illustrations of just some of our wild plants. Both the maximum heights and flowering times are included (these are also in the complete list at the end), but I stress that these are approximate. Heights can vary enormously depending on weather and soil conditions. The same is true of flowering times, where location can also play a great part. Our accelerating climate change, or global warming, is already causing havoc among some species.

Perennials include bulbs, corms, tubers, rhizomes and others. There is no category for 'shrubs', since the distinction between trees, shrubs and perennials is often very blurred. The eventual approximate heights are a better guide, especially for small gardens.

I have very much enlarged the flowers in some of the photographs. This is deliberate, as a much closer look at some of our apparently insignificant flowers of only two or three millimetres often reveals an astonishing wealth of detail and beauty frequently not found in larger flowers. All the pictures taken have been of plants growing in their natural habitats.

In some cases I have given the animal or insect that is particularly dependent or attracted by a plant, but every single wild species is useful to someone, somewhere.

The complete list of native species of the Botanical Society of the British Isles (BSBI) follows. To this we have added other details as to type, height, flowering times and very brief details of habitats. In both this and the former section, botanical names take precedence and only one common name (the one allocated by the BSBI) is given. Common names often cause confusion: different counties have different names, and some wild plants have twenty or more all steeped in history, folklore, medicine and much else. I hope they will continue to be used in books about wild plants rather than only in ones on how to grow them such as this. They are a fascinating study in themselves.

1

Getting Started

THE FOLLOWING CHAPTER TELLS YOU
everything you need to know about starting
out with native plants, from buying and
collecting seeds to preparing the ground,
sowing and much more.

IF YOU WERE PRESENTED WITH A VIRGIN PLOT OF LAND THE SIZE OF AN average suburban garden, what would you do with it? I am assuming you want to fill it with native plants and attract wildlife. Here are some features you might consider: ◆ *a tiny woodland* (a few trees and shrubs are enough) ◆ *a woodland verge* ◆ a *pond* with a surrounding wetland area ◆ *plenty of sunny spaces* for flowers and/or *a meadow* ◆ *a native hedge* ◆ *a pile or two of logs* (home for beetles and others).

However, such a scenario is very unlikely unless you have just bought a brand-new house. But the above are habitats you should bear in mind when turning your existing, probably well-stocked, garden into one for wildlife. You need not do everything at once – small areas can be cleared and gradually turned over to wild plants and in a very few years you could have a totally native garden buzzing with wildlife.

If you do not already have a pond, I would strongly urge you to find a place for one immediately, however small. Even try to get some areas waterlogged (see page 36). There are not only an immense variety of plants that you can grow in and around ponds which will not grow elsewhere, but such an area will very quickly attract large numbers of wildlife: small creatures such as water boatmen and pond skaters will almost immediately inhabit the pond and the larvae of many beautiful moths rely on pond plants. Frogs, toads, dragonflies, and others will follow – even fish have been known to appear out of nowhere! It will also give birds and small mammals a source of water essential at all times and may be lifesaving during droughts. If your garden is small, you should aim for habitats to attract mainly birds, insects and invertebrates – the larger mammals such as badgers, foxes and even deer are wonderful but would probably cause havoc. So, if you do not already have a pond, maybe this is the time to build one. There are many books and leaflets on how to construct ponds of various sizes.

Always remember that nothing in this book has to be on a large scale, even if some of the pictures give that impression. An astonishing biodiversity can be achieved in very small gardens.

There is another important factor that you should consider at the outset: you should resist the temptation to use any chemicals, especially herbicides and pesticides, and I will elaborate on this later.

It will help when establishing wild plants to know whether your soil is clay, chalky, sandy or peaty: you can usually tell by the look and feel. The type of soil will play quite a large part in which species will grow well. It is also helpful to establish whether your soil is neutral, acid or alkaline. There are very simple soil-testing kits on the market that will help you analyse the soil. It is logical that species native to a particular soil (or a combination thereof) will grow there much better. However, there is no hard-and-fast rule – many other plants will grow in a soil not necessarily endemic to them. You will just have to experiment: if you find a plant persistently languishing in your soil, do not force it to grow by producing all kinds of 'additives'. It is much better to find something else that will flourish.

You can find out which native plants grow in your area by going to the *Flora for Fauna* website (www.nhm.ac.uk/fff). Simply key in your postcode and you will be given a very comprehensive list of plants.

One thing to remember is that you cannot change the profile of your soil: the addition of any amounts of peat substitutes will not make your soil acid. (Do not add or buy real peat, because its extraction only deprives other wildlife of its natural habitat.) Nor can you make clay calcareous by adding chalk and so on. However, these additives may initially help to establish certain plants.

The information on the following pages will explain the various options open to you for starting out with native plants.

Experiment

A fun experiment is to dig up a small area, one or two square metres, to a depth of 50–60 cm. Bring the soil from that depth to the surface and see what happens. Maybe nothing untoward – just more of what you already have! On the other hand, you may be surprised to find plants coming up that you have never seen in the garden. Seeds of most native species remain viable in the soil for many years, even centuries, just waiting for light and the right conditions to pop up and flower! Who knows? They may have become buried when your house was built and have lain dormant ever since! Whatever does come up is almost certainly indigenous to your area.

You might also try growing a 'mini' meadow on a small piece of ground. This might help you decide which species to 'cultivate'. You could choose a grassland, arable, wet or woodland meadow (see chapter 2).

Buying native plants and seeds

The easiest but also the most expensive way of establishing native plants is to start by buying them in plugs or pots. Wild plants are not necessarily

Below: A pile of logs or any deadwood in the garden is invaluable for biodiversity. It not only provides shelter for countless invertebrates, but in time mosses, lichens and fungi may grow,

cheaper than their cultivated counterparts. But it may also be the best introduction to them and you will probably have a very high-percentage success rate. As soon as you get the plants, either pot them on or plant out straightaway (see the sections on preparing ground and planting out).

Right: Spiked Star-of-
Bethlehem
(*Ornithogalum
pyrenaicum*). This
particular plant was
growing along the
side of a very busy
road in Sussex. It is
not a very common
plant and normally
grows in woodlands
in the Bath area –
hence its other
name, Bath
Asparagus. The tall
stems used to be
eaten as a delicacy
while still in bud –
just like asparagus.
However, it shows
that roadsides can be
good for collecting
seeds, but maybe not
ones as busy as this!

Collecting your own seeds

The cheapest way to start out with native plants is to collect and sow your own seeds. This may be more difficult and time-consuming, but is great fun and much more rewarding in the long run, and gives you a lot of experience of wildlife and insight into how wild plants grow.

Seeds will ripen at various times from early summer to late autumn. It largely depends on when they flowered, which can vary considerably from area to area, and in what sort of location they are flowering. Plants in full sun, facing south, tend to come out earlier than ones facing north, and others may be growing in a microclimate created by hedges, shrubs or walls.

Since it is much easier to identify plants in flower, the best thing is to locate those you want while they are flowering and then go back four to eight weeks later to collect the seeds.

All wild plants are protected from uprooting by the Wildlife and Countryside Act 1981. The species listed in Schedule 8 of this Act (very rare and endangered plants) are even protected from seed collection without a permit. It would be wise to get a copy of this Act – it can be viewed on the Internet. Failure to comply with it can result in prosecution.

You should take along a good book on identifying wild plants. Unfortunately, most of them include plants growing throughout Britain and Europe, and it is sometimes difficult to establish which are native to Britain and which have been introduced and therefore alien. The list at the end of the book is the best indicator.

Where and how to collect

With the exception of Schedule 8, you can, theoretically, collect seed from any woodlands, meadows or land open to the public. In practice, you should not go to nature reserves or any protected areas such as SSSIs (Sites of Special Scientific Interest) without first consulting the warden. You may be taking seeds from the very plant or plants that have made the site special! If the land is private, you must always get permission from the owner. In my experience, permission is rarely refused once you tell the owner the purpose of your visit and assure him/her that great care will be taken while collecting.

Parks and woodland areas that are open to the public are a good source, as are the verges of public

Garden centres and nurseries everywhere now sell 'wild' flower seeds and plants. If you buy from them, insist that they are of true native origin. Unfortunately, all too often they are not: sometimes they are seeds or bulbs that have been collected from abroad. There are many instances where indigenous overseas sites have been all but denuded of lovely colonies of plants. Even in Britain sites have suffered frequently from wholesale exploitation by commercial concerns. More often, the plants have been hybridized or genetically 'tampered' with to make them grow bigger, brighter and better, demanded by a general public who want more instant, bigger and better results in everything. Even species with the same name but collected from abroad will have subtle differences that can affect wildlife.

At the back of the book you will find a sourcebook of the names and addresses of growers and nurseries who can guarantee the origins of their seeds and plants – all collected legally – so, if at all possible, buy from them to ensure that you are getting truly native plants.

footpaths. The Ramblers' Association should be able to provide maps of the paths in your area. Your local Wildlife Trust may also be able to help you source particular species since most keep botanical records for the county.

One of the best places to look is along road verges and hedgerows especially on small country roads. Often these marked the boundary, some many centuries ago, between private woods and land. Many will have had ancient woodland or meadows on either side and will therefore contain the remnants of the wild plants that grew there, despite the fact that modern farmland now flanks the road on either side. Some of our most ancient trees that

escaped the woodsman's axe are sometimes found along these boundaries, as well as many native flowers. Wild meadows and downlands are also excellent. Another good source is cemeteries, especially those attached to old churches.

I was taken by Bruce Middleton to a site where the Spiked Star-of-Bethlehem (*Ornithogalum pyrenaicum*) grows (see opposite). In this case, it was along a narrow strip of land with a busy road on one side and a paved walkway on the other! It was something of a miracle that this plant (uncommon and protected) had survived – doubtless due only to pressure on the local council not to cut the strip either side before early autumn!

Above: This small patch from a woodland bank could provide a wealth of seeds. In flower are Bluebell, Greater Stitchwort and Primrose. About to flower are Yellow Archangel (centre) and Red Campion (bottom right). Also present is Rosebay Willowherb (beautiful but invasive) as well as Bramble and Stinging Nettle.

When you have decided where and when to collect seeds, you should go armed with the following:

◆ Plenty of plastic or paper bags/envelopes
◆ String and/or bag ties
◆ Labels and pen
◆ Holdall in which to put the bags of seeds
◆ Suitable footwear, especially if going into wet fields, ditches or bogs
◆ Strong trousers to protect legs from brambles and stinging nettles
◆ Scissors or secateurs
◆ Pocket-sized wild-flower book to help identification

The best time to go is late afternoon on a sunny day, when plants should be dry and moisture will not collect inside bags as it would if seeds were collected in the midday sun. Try not to collect seeds in wet weather, but if you are caught unawares and it starts raining, get the seeds and heads home as soon as possible, and spread them out or hang them up to dry.

When collecting seeds, observe the following:

◆ Check seeds are ripe (leave if white or green)
◆ Take only a small quantity
◆ Never take the only seed head
◆ Never pull up any plant
◆ Disturb the surrounding plants as little as possible
◆ Try not to trample on soil too much – it will compact it and inhibit growth
◆ If taking seeds from tall spikes of flowers, take only the bottom ones – leave the rest to ripen

As soon as you get home, do the following:

◆ Lay out individual seeds to dry on plates or trays
◆ Lay out or hang up seed heads in a dry room on or above a tray. 'Exploding' seed pods should be covered to avoid losing seeds
◆ As soon as seed heads are dry, shake or extract seeds
◆ Bag up and label seeds with species name and date and store seed in a dry cool place

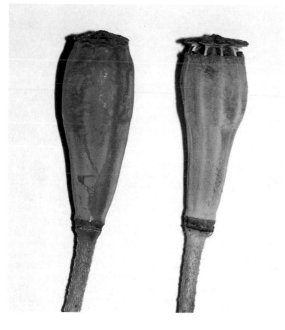

Above: It is far better to collect seeds that are really ripe. 'Green' ones may dry out and ripen at home but it is not certain whether they will be viable. The pods of ripe seeds will very often identify themselves by turning brown and looking very dry. If you are not certain and the pod is still closed, open it up to check – unripe seeds will normally be white or green and soft, while ripe ones will have hardened and turned brown or black. Some seeds are almost like dust and difficult to judge whether they are ripe or not, but colour is usually a good indication.

Left: When collecting seeds, do make sure you take only ripe ones and never take all the available seeds of any particular plant. Should the plant be an annual, you will deprive that area of future flowers; if it is a perennial, you will prevent its further spread. In the picture it is very obvious which pods are ripe. Often it is easier to pick whole pods, in which case lay them out on a tray in a dry place, and the seeds will soon separate.

Above: This picture shows Meadow Clary (*Salvia pratensis*), where the ripe seeds are very black. The other shows Common Poppy (*Papaver rhoeas*). Although you cannot see the poppy seeds, the ripe head has turned brown and if you shake it the seeds will rattle.

Left: Sometimes it is easier to pick a whole stem or head of seeds rather than try to get them into bags on site. In this case, hang them up in a dry place as soon as you get home. You will soon see seeds dropping down onto the tray or paper below.

Preparing the ground and planning

At the beginning of this chapter, I said that, if you are going to grow wild flowers for wildlife, you should resist the temptation to use any chemicals. The longer you can do this before starting out the better. The reasons are many and some not all that obvious.

Chemicals will kill off the insects and plants on which other wildlife depends. In a wild garden one has to tolerate just about everything – many so-called pests: slugs, snails and others, as well as some thistles, nettles and docks. If some 'weeds' get out of

Right: A piece of ground covered with plastic and anchored down with logs.

hand they should be dug out or suppressed with mulches. You will find that most pests will be controlled biologically by their natural predators, although in some cases you may have to give your small plants a helping hand (see Pests and diseases, page 23). Look at it from the wildlife point of view and the decision will be much easier. Our declining songbirds, especially thrushes, depend on slugs, snails and others for their main food source. The larvae of many insects such as butterflies and moths depend on 'weeds'. One could write volumes on how indigenous flora and fauna totally depend on each other for food and shelter. By growing native plants for wildlife, you should aim to create an ecosystem in which everything from the tiniest soil creatures (some invisible) to the larger mammals and birds will thrive.

Another reason for not using chemicals is not all that apparent. There are fungi in the soil, most invisible, called *mycorrhiza*, on which almost all plants in the natural world depend. They are present all over the planet, even at the north and south poles, and they form a truly symbiotic relationship with plants in whose roots and stems

they grow. The plants' roots supply the *mycorrhiza* with carbohydrates necessary to their growth, and in return the fungi supply plants with essential nutrients such as nitrogen, phosphorus, trace elements and minerals, as well as water. Many plants, orchids for example, cannot even germinate without the presence of the right *mycorrhiza*, yet alone grow into strong healthy specimens. It is said that 90 per cent of the world's plants depend on these fungi. But the fungi are also very susceptible to chemicals, the use of which will kill them and make the establishment of wild plants more difficult, and your garden may not easily become a haven for all kinds of wildlife. *Mycorrhiza* may take many, many years to re-establish themselves.

For the last half-century or more chemicals have been poured into the soil and seemed essential for the life-giving production of food. Now, many are questioning the efficacy and wisdom of this practice, even for food. That is not the concern of this book, but I guarantee your plants and resultant wildlife will be immeasurably better off and in time you will find such gardening infinitely more rewarding and exciting.

If you are a meticulous gardener, you may have to change your habits and attitudes when creating and maintaining a garden that is not only full of indigenous plants but is attracting and sustaining wildlife. Apart from not using chemicals, stop excessive weeding and being too tidy! Why rake up autumn leaves unless they are on a paved area? They will nourish plants and for a time make a hideaway for some small creature. Do not automatically pull up plants you do not recognize without first identifying them and making sure that they are really not an attribute.

You may want to clear a lawn or large area completely to make way for a meadow or border. You could abandon mowing an existing lawn and see what happens. I did this and was hugely rewarded (see page 26), but the chances are that lawn grasses (especially if they were fertilized) will be coarse and will overpower wild plants. In the long run it is probably better to start from scratch, and this is essential if you want to create a border rather than a meadow.

Clearing the ground need not be backbreaking digging and forking: cut any existing vegetation to ground level and cover the area with a light-excluding mulch. Two of the best are thick, black commercial plastic (not normally the kind sold in garden centres) and old, pure-wool carpets (do not use synthetic fibres, since they will only break up and make a mess). The mulches will have to be anchored down with bricks or something heavy that will prevent the wind blowing them away.

Large pieces of cardboard anchored down are also good light excluders. Cardboard does not last very long – it will soon rot with no harm to the soil.

The longer you can leave the light-excluding mulch the better, but a few months should be sufficient for all but the most persistent 'weeds'. Do not uncover the soil until you are absolutely ready either to plant or sow seeds. You could also use a rotavator, but this would still leave many grasses and other plants in the soil.

Sowing seeds

In nature, plants would just drop their seeds when ripe: birds or wind might scatter them and in due course they would germinate – some in autumn and some the following spring. You now have to decide when, where and how to sow the seeds you have either collected or purchased. Personally, I would always sow them in late autumn around November time.

Seeds that have been stored very soon become dormant, and this 'dormancy' has to be 'broken', or, more simply, the seeds have to be 'woken up'. Different plants require different conditions to break their dormancy: some, especially harder ones need to be subjected to either heat or frost or both. When you subject a seed to heat or cold, it is called cold or warm stratification.

Cold stratification involves putting the seeds into a refrigerator (not in the ice box) and keeping them there in a temperature below 5°C for two or three weeks. Sometimes, you can actually see roots emerging from the pods, in which case they should be sown immediately.

Warm stratification requires a temperature of 15–18°C, so almost any room in the house that does not get too hot or too cold will do. In extreme cases some seeds have to be subjected to fire or very high temperatures, but this normally only applies to plants that come in a casing – such as fir cones – which have to be burst open to expel the seeds.

Other seeds, usually very tough ones, may have to be subjected to scarification in order to induce them to better germinate. This could mean either

soaking them in water or rubbing the outer shell with emery paper, or even 'nicking' a corner with a sharp knife.

All this may sound laborious and can be quite complicated. However, the good news is that none of it is necessary when starting out to grow native plants. I mention it so that you will not be disappointed if some seeds do not germinate immediately and maybe think you have done something wrong. Wild plants have minds of their own and can be tricky and wayward in their habits. Even with professional handling, some seeds, especially trees and shrubs, may take several years before they decide to germinate. In the wild, plants really like to grow in their own time and place without being forced, so why should they behave differently in your garden?

I have also touched on stratification and scarification, because I think they are the best reasons for sowing seeds in late autumn/early winter. Nature, in the form of wind, rain, frosts and snow, will perform all these functions. Surely it is better to harness nature to do some of the work for you?

Sowing seeds in autumn/winter does allow a longer time for predators at the leanest time of year

Left: A piece of ground with plastic pulled back showing that the patch is not yet totally clear of grass and 'weeds'. Do not forget that the roots of some persistent plants, like docks and stinging nettles, will regrow unless the area remains covered for a very long time – maybe as long as two years.

(birds, insects and small mammals) to disturb and consume seeds. Also, the ground may be subjected to extreme weather conditions in the form of floods, in which case you may find plants growing in a totally different place! With climate changes you may not get any frosts at all until late spring, when tender seedlings have emerged only to be blackened or shrivelled up! I have no doubt, however, that you will succeed, even in the worst conditions.

Below: Part of a tray showing Dark Mullein seedlings. Before they emerge, always make sure the soil is kept damp: either stand tray in shallow water, or cover with glass or clear plastic, but remove as soon as plants germinate. If you leave them covered and standing in sunlight the seedlings will be scorched.

Below: Sowing seeds evenly direct from a packet into open ground can be difficult and you may end up with clusters of plants and bare patches of ground. If you mix the seeds with fine sand or sawdust, it will distribute them more evenly.

Sowing seeds in pots and boxes

If you intend to sow seeds in pots or boxes, mix up some garden soil with white or sharp sand (only if the soil is really heavy), and add leaf mould and/or garden compost. About one-third of the latter to soil should be adequate. You can also purchase organic seed compost from most garden centres. Sow the seeds thinly and press down firmly. Larger seeds should be sown to their own depth. Make sure you label everything. You may not recognize all the small seedlings and end up planting them out in the wrong place! If pots and boxes are kept outside, they normally don't need watering during the winter months. If it is in danger of drying out, a piece of glass or clear plastic spread over the top will help retain moisture. Keep pots and boxes outside at all times, no matter when they were sown.

Sowing directly into the ground

If you are sowing directly into the ground, prepare an area as described on pages 16 and 17. Break up the soil as much as possible and make a fine tilth. Sow seeds as evenly and thinly as possible and press them into the ground. It is not easy to sow tiny seeds evenly, but mixing them with some fine sand or sawdust may help.

Planting bulbs and rhizomes

If you purchase bulbs such as snowdrops, bluebells or wild daffodils, plant these at least 8–10 cm deep. They will grow if planted in much shallower ground, but at this depth they are far less likely to be eaten by mice and other rodents. It is surprising how deep you can plant bulbs and yet they still find their way into the light. When growing bulbous plants or orchids from seed, bear in mind that most will take two to four years or more before they will flower.

Below left and right: There are several kinds of dibber, some quite sophisticated, and even ones that save you the trouble of bending down! The one in the picture on the left is a plain wooden one that can be used anywhere. Just make a sufficiently deep hole, pop in the bulb and fill in with soil. Note that the small bulbs are already sprouting (below right), so make sure you plant them as soon as purchased. These bulbs were Star-of-Bethlehem (*Ornithogalum angustifolium*).

Above: If planting bulbs to naturalize in an existing lawn, you can use a conventional dibber, or cut out a piece of turf about 8–10 cm deep, as shown in the top picture. Put three or four bulbs in the bottom and replace the piece of turf. In this case the bulbs were Spring Squill (*Scilla verna*).

Above: If you buy plants, many of them will come as rhizomes, such as this Lily-of-the-Valley (*Convallaria majalis*). These will have to be planted in a shallow trench, and then covered with sufficient earth so that the bud is just below the surface. Note the second single bud already growing out of the parent.

Left: As soon as plantlets are large enough to handle, transplant into plugs or small pots. No special tools are required – just loosen the roots and lift with a pencil or small tool (in this case the actual plant label was used), and press into the plug filled with soil and then water. Do not forget to label the batch of plugs or pots.

Right: Seedlings can either be transplanted into small pots as seen here, or moved into plugs.

Potting on, thinning and planting out

By spring, both the seeds in boxes and pots and those outside should be germinating. (Spring sowings may be a little later, depending on the weather.) The exact time will vary from area to area. I would not thin the seedlings growing in the ground, but those in pots and boxes should be pricked out as soon as they are large enough to handle. Put them into small individual pots, and as soon as they are growing well either plant out or pot on into larger containers. I like to have the plants strong and sturdy before putting them into the 'wild' – especially prized ones or ones that proved difficult in the past. Any move seems to set back a plant temporarily and maybe weakens it, thus making it more prone to pests and diseases.

When planting out, try to disturb the roots as little as possible – loosen the roots and soil only if the plant is pot-bound with its roots tightly curled round the pot.

Unless you have managed to sow seeds thinly and evenly outside, many may come up in a bunch. You can certainly thin them and plant some in empty spaces, but these plants will almost certainly be weaker than those left undisturbed. You can also leave them to sort themselves out.

An experiment of my own

When I learned I was going to write this book, it was already spring, and the book had to be finished early the following year. Nevertheless, against all my instincts, I decided to experiment sowing a number of wild species that spring. I decided to put half the seeds of a species in trays and the other half on a cleared piece of ground in the vegetable garden. I made no effort to give any of them special treatment or to protect them.

The results were mixed if not disastrous! Only four species out of ten germinated in the boxes – namely Wild Thyme, Wild Basil, Wild Mignonette and one of the two poppy species. Out of these four, only two survived (Wild Basil and Wild Mignonette). The others were all eaten by birds or mice. Other seeds may still be there waiting to germinate another year.

The ones sown in the garden fared a little better. Two sturdy Tree Mallows emerged (which I soon put into pots), as well as all the four that had germinated in the trays. You could hardly call a 50 per cent success rate good, although I must admit that one, Bog Asphodel, should have had special treatment. I did put it in a holeless tray with water and sphagnum moss, but, alas, the tray dried out on several occasions. The Welsh Poppy made no appearance at all; the Yellow Horned-poppy was eaten; all the Quaking Grass seed was, I think, consumed by mice. An enormous number of other 'weeds' also emerged – not all of them unwelcome but they were not what I had sown!

On the other hand, I had sown a box of Travellers' Joy or Old Man's Beard (*Clematis vitalba*) collected from a roadside hedge the previous autumn and left it out all winter. Despite being disturbed by mice and birds, I now have a

large number of potted-up plants ready to go out in the autumn.

Wild Basil belongs to the Labiate family and the flowers have that typical gaping look as if pleading for insects to visit. At first glance it could be mistaken for a Red Dead-nettle (*Lamium purpureum*). It has a pleasant scent and certainly attracts a host of small insects. It is edible and although it can be used for flavouring various dishes, it has nothing like the pungent taste and strong flavour of the basil used with pasta. It grows mainly in the south and east of England and is scarce elsewhere.

Above, left and right: This is the Tree Mallow I had sown in the spring. By the autumn it had grown into a sizeable plant with good roots, which had to be loosened before putting it into a large hole. It is important to loosen the roots without damaging them before planting out regardless whether the plant is in a tiny or large pot. I recently bought some trees that had been put into large pots. Some of them were so pot-bound that it was impossible to do this. Although they lived through the first year, they hardly put on any growth.

Above and right: Here are some of the Wild Basil (*Clinopodium vulgare*) seeds that I sowed in the vegetable garden. Contrary to expectations, they fought their way through all the other 'weeds' that came up in the plot, and both they and the ones I had sown in trays and potted on flowered most of the summer.

Growing orchids

Many wild orchids were and are on the brink of extinction largely due to loss of habitat and, regrettably, due to people's attempts to dig them up illegally and grow them in gardens (usually without success). However, during the last few years enormous strides have been made in growing orchids from seed. This has been largely due to research involving universities, Kew Gardens and

Right: Early-purple Orchid (*Orchis mascula*) growing wild on a woodland verge.

specialist horticulturalists. Their work has saved many orchids from extinction and the result is that more and more species are becoming available in plugs and pots from certain outlets.

Orchids are exciting and fascinating plants and I am sure many of you will be anxious to have them in the garden. Growing them from seed is still highly specialized and not easy, so I would advise that you initially purchase small plants (some suppliers are given at the back of the book). Be warned: these are not cheap and success is not guaranteed. They should be planted out in the right place (research their requirements well before spending a lot of money) with all the soil in which they come. This is important, because the soil and roots will contain the right mycorrhizal fungi with which the particular orchid is associated. Rather than plant them in isolation, put them with some of the plants with which they are associated in the wild. They will appreciate some garden compost, but do not use any chemicals.

The genera *Dactylorhiza* and *Orchis* are probably the best to start with in a garden, and many

stunning different varieties are available. I am lucky to have large colonies of the Common Spotted Orchid (*Dactylorhiza fuchsii*) and Early Purple (*Orchis mascula*) growing in the woods, and the former seem to appear almost anywhere. They are all self-sown. I have never tried to collect seed and sow it (something I must rectify). Recently, I did buy two species in pots, which so far have shown no signs of establishing themselves – I probably planted them in the wrong place!

This said, a friend of mine, Mike Mullis, who grows and sells wild plants, has very successfully established the Common Spotted (*Dactylorhiza fuchsii*) and Pyramidal Orchid (*Anacamptis pyramidalis*) on his ground. He says he achieved this by merely scattering the seeds in appropriate places, but I am sure he is being modest when he says, 'Establishing wild orchids from seed isn't as difficult as you might think although you do need to be very patient, as it can take up to five or six years or more before flowers first appear. Perhaps the trickiest bit is acquiring some wild seed to start with. You also need the right sort of unimproved planting area or growing habitat and perhaps a little luck along the way.'

He continues, 'Although successful means of germinating orchids have been developed using cultures and other laboratory techniques, I prefer the less-than-scientific view that the symbiotic fungus is either present or absent in the local soil – in theory a fifty–fifty chance! Quite often, though, this fungus is naturally present in the ground, especially if the soil is unimproved, i.e. there have been no added nutrients in the form of compost, fertilizers, chemicals, phosphates or artificial additives.

'Orchid seed is dustlike and tends to blow away if sown in anything more than a very light breeze. Sow the seed very sparingly and straight onto the surface of any suitable bare soil in very still, calm weather conditions, ideally in the autumn. The seed needs to be scattered from just a couple of inches above the ground, so you really need to be on your knees to do this – there's no point in wasting precious seed if you try to sow from a standing position unless you can easily touch your toes!

'Rain later in the day, or gentle watering is ideal for washing seed naturally into areas of bare soil,' Mike advises. 'The ground should then be left undisturbed and unenriched, although grassland can still be cut at least annually as long as all cuttings are raked up and removed.

'The first single, spotted leaf or shoot of a Common Spotted Orchid may appear within eighteen months of sowing, but it may take longer. It will probably take another two or three years before the first flower appears – in June – but with each passing year the plant develops stronger leaf growth and a bigger fleshy, tuber type of root or rhizome. I've managed to establish quite a large number of Common Spotted Orchids from seed in damp grassland and in damp, bare clay/sandstone – on former agricultural ground – at my site over the last few years.

'On a drier, well-drained, more alkaline grass bank on site,' Mike adds, 'I've also managed to get a number of Pyramid Orchids, or *Anacamptis pyramidalis*, to establish from seed over a similar time period and using identical sowing techniques.'

There is a very useful website (*www. reallywildflowers.co.uk/documents/orchids.doc*) which will give you invaluable information about establishing orchids in your garden. There is also a recently published and extremely useful book, *Orchids of the British Isles*, by Michael Foley and Sidney Clarke (Griffin Press), which not only gives information about every British species but also gives guidelines on how to grow them.

Pests and diseases

By now you may have gleaned that there is nothing much you should do about pests and diseases except avoid chemicals.

In the wild, plants are rarely decimated by pests. The worst culprits are usually rabbits and deer, but most of you are unlikely to get them in your garden. However, when you are growing wild plants under 'forced' conditions, problems can occur in the early stages. Seedlings seem to be particularly vulnerable when transplanted.

If slugs and snails become a real problem (especially with expensive orchids), you can protect the plants with one of the organic slug deterrents available in garden centres. Alternatively you can set your own traps by putting beer into small containers and partially sinking them into the ground (slugs seem particularly attracted to beer, which must bring them a euphoric death!). You can also control them biologically by purchasing nematodes, but these will be effective for only a few

weeks. By far the best way is to encourage the right birds, frogs and hedgehogs to make their home in the garden – their diet consists mainly of slugs, snails and others.

On the whole, nature seems to find its own balances, so that no one pest gets the upper hand. An onslaught of a particular pest, such as aphids, seems simultaneously to produce a host of predators – in this case wasps, hoverflies, ladybirds or others. Highly cultivated plants in the form of hybrids or exotic imports are often prone to endless problems. A good example is roses: there are countless 'cures' on the market against aphids, rust, mildew and other problems from which most roses seem to suffer. Wild roses, however, never seem to have such problems, despite the fact that, apart from supplying countless insects with nectar, they are also the major food plant for many moth larvae, and the rosehips supply many birds with much-needed food in the middle of winter. In fact, wild roses seed freely and can become a nuisance.

Extreme weather conditions or a totally wrong environment or soil can weaken plants and lay them open to pests and diseases. The worst of these are late frosts and drought. There is nothing you can do about the former, but plants frequently recover despite looking black and dead. Personally, I rarely water plants in the garden – as long as there is plenty of humus in the soil and there are mulches on the surface, I leave them to fend for themselves. But can anyone really predict the effect of climate change?

As far as diseases are concerned, the same principles apply and I would not attempt any 'cures'. It is rare that any one disease completely wipes out plants in the wild. If it does, it is usually one that comes from abroad, such as Dutch Elm disease.

I hope you have found some of the above helpful and will succeed with native plants. Always remember that some seeds do not necessarily germinate the first year and that some plants just may not like your soil. You are bound to succeed with some, and with patience and perseverance you will have many that will not only give you a sense of achievement, but endless joy and fascination. What better satisfaction than to see the results of the biodiversity you have created in the garden, a host of plants of all hues, large and tiny, and to watch and listen to the birds and observe a flourishing myriad insects, invertebrates and small mammals?

Meadows

2

ORIGINALLY A MEADOW WAS A FIELD
from which cattle were excluded at certain
times of the year so that hay could be cut for
winter feeds. But there are many types of
meadow, including grassland, arable,
woodland and wetland. There are others, but
only these four are covered in this chapter.
You could establish any or all of them in your
garden. You do not require large areas of land:
a few square metres would be adequate.

Above: This is part of my own lawn, which, some years ago, I decided not to cut. Imagine my astonishment and delight when a mass or Common Spotted Orchids (*Dactylorhiza fuchsii*) appeared as well as much else! I have to admit that the lawn is next to an ancient woodland, so do not expect this to happen to your lawn except under such special circumstances. However, seeds of these orchids can now be purchased, so why not have a go?

When I embarked on this book, I envisaged photographing various gardens that had been populated with native plants to give you an idea what your garden might eventually turn into. I found many lovely 'wild' gardens, but, unfortunately, garden centres or nurseries had sold the owners many plants under the label 'native' that were not truly so. Many were cultivars or even hybrids, so, rather than confuse you (this book is, after all, about British native wild plants), I decided to illustrate various types of meadows. Some were created by sowing and planting, and some are cameos of what nature had produced of its own accord.

Grassland meadows

Unfortunately, due to burgeoning farmland and modern practices, most natural meadows have largely disappeared (it is said to be by as much as 97 per cent), but they can be a rich colourful collection of flowers and grasses that are not only stunning to look at but will also attract and sustain large numbers of birds and insects. It can also be a good way to get to know some of our native species. Fortunately many NGOs (nongovernmental organizations) as well as government organizations are now working to recreate some of our meadows before they completely disappear. Most of you will be able to create only a micro image of some of these meadows, but what better satisfaction than to be able to observe them daily and throughout the seasons?

There are two ways you can establish a grassland meadow: either stop mowing an existing part of your lawn and see what happens or start from scratch. In time you will probably get a collection of wild flowers and grasses, but in practice some of the grasses may be overpowering and will have to be removed. Specially sown plants can always be grown and planted out in the bare patches, but if the soil is rich the unwanted 'weeds' will continually have to be removed.

I did not mow part of my lawn for a whole year, and the following spring I was greeted with the exciting sight of literally a 'meadow' of Common Spotted Orchids (*Dactylorhiza fuchsii*). Later in the year Bird's-foot Trefoil (*Lotus corniculatus*), various clovers, Meadow Buttercup, Bugle, Knapweed and others appeared. Recently several clumps of Snakeshead Fritillary (*Fritillaria meleagris*) also emerged. That particular part of the lawn was originally damp and moss-ridden. So far I have not deliberately introduced any other species. The area is usually cut in late summer/early autumn.

The alternative and probably the best way to grow a grassland meadow is to start from scratch and prepare a piece of ground as described on page 16. Buy a packet of meadow seeds (normally consisting of a few species of grass and ten or more flowers) and sow these in either autumn or spring. Maybe some of the flowers will not come up the first year, but may do so in subsequent years. Keep out all the invasive and overpowering 'weeds'. Make sure that the mixture is true native and contains Yellow-rattle (*Rhinanthus minor*, see page 88) and, if it does not, buy some separately. You can also make your own choice of species and sow them almost any perennials that prefer open sunny sites are suitable, although those that prefer your type of soil will probably be the most vigorous. You should sow seed mixtures at the rate of approximately 2–4 grams per square metre. Yet another alternative is to buy plugs or pots of selective species.

As soon as your meadow reaches about 20 cm, it should be cut down to 5–6 cm. In subsequent years it will have to be cut at least once, or even two or three times, depending on the species growing. If, for instance, you have established Cowslips (*Primula veris*) or similar early flowering species, the meadow should be cut as soon as seeds have set – normally between mid- and late June. This will still allow other species to flower later in summer. Another cut should be made in early autumn. The normal practice is to remove all cuttings so that the soil does not become too fertile and unwanted coarse grasses and other 'weeds' do not take over. However, some plants appreciate a bit of extra 'food', and cuttings have the added advantage that they produce a mulch that retains moisture in extreme dry conditions. In a small area you could remove any unwanted species by hand.

The choice of plants is enormous – in fact any flower or grass that prefers sun and does not like to be waterlogged is suitable for a grassland meadow. Some species will overlap the different kinds of meadows such as Cuckoo Flower (*Cardamine pratensis*), primroses and others. Grasses, as the name implies, are an integral part of any grassland meadow but it is important that they are the right kind – coarse and invasive grasses will only overpower the plants that you hope will produce a glorious display of colour. The grasses to avoid are couch grass (*Elytrigia repens*, formerly *Agropyron repens*) and others in the same family; Rye grass (*Lolium perenne*) is not good, nor are Cock's Foot and Tall Fescue (*Dactylis glomerata* and *Festuca arundinacea*).

The ones that are desirable include bent grasses (*Agrostis spp.*), the meadow grasses (*Poa spp.*), some of the fescues (*Festuca spp.*) and Crested Dog's-tail. Sweet Vernal grass (*Anthoxanthum odoratum*) will give you that sweetly intoxicating scent of hay when it is cut, because it contains coumarin.

Left: A little area of grass that shows promising signs for a meadow. There do not appear to be too many grasses and the plants, although all fairly common, would provide a good start. They include Self-heal (*Prunella vulgaris*), trefoils and clovers.

The pictures on the following pages should give you an idea of what can be grown in a grassland meadow. There are, of course, many more species that can be included, but exactly in which combination may well depend on your location and the type of soil. As with everything concerning wild plants, it is best to experiment.

In the picture on the left are various Fescues. The picture on the right shows some Yorkshire Fog (*Holcus lanatus*). It is not a very good idea to introduce Yorkshire Fog in the first two or three years, since it could become invasive. I think it is a stunning grass and could be planted on its own in the garden. When in bud, the plumes are red or various shades of pink that open up into a wonderful haze of seeds and flowers – presumably that is where it gets the 'fog' from in its name.

Right: I found this small piece of meadow among much larger shrubs and scrub. It sadly illustrates what a wonderful sight this could have been had it covered a large area of several hectares. The brilliant yellow of Lady's Bedstraw (*Galium verum*) is interspersed with Black Knapweed (*Centaurea nigra*), various clovers and grasses, and just a hint of trefoils.

Left: I found this natural collection of plants, consisting largely of mallows and campions, on some waste ground near a car park. It was on the side of the road and in places you could see the tracks of cars. Despite this, a remarkable and striking collection of plants had emerged. The poppies' seeds must either have been in their first year or been disturbed by the cars. If you sow a meadow on fairly clear ground, you could, in the first year, include some of the cornfield annuals such as these poppies, corn marigold, cornflower and others. It is highly unlikely they would reappear in the second year.

Left: This is a little window from a grassland meadow managed by Emorsgate Seeds. In this picture the delicate Fairy Flax (*Linum catharticum*) dominates. You can also see Clover, Buttercup and Yellow Rattle among the grasses. Both Fairy Flax and Yellow-rattle are annuals.

Above: These poppies
are growing in a
strip of farmland at
the edge of a field
of corn.

Arable or cornfield meadows

These are the plants that used to grow naturally among the corn, but modern farm practices have made them virtually extinct in this habitat. They include many of the plants (usually referred to as arable weeds) whose native origin is now in dispute, but since most have been here for centuries I think the question is rather academic.

These meadows are very different from grassland meadows. In the first place, a grassland meadow consists mainly of perennials, and in a cornfield they are all annuals. In order to germinate, the seeds require the soil to be disturbed every year – something that occurred naturally when farmers ploughed the fields before sowing corn. These annuals include flowers that are quite breathtaking when growing en masse: the awesome reds of Poppies (*Papaver rhoeas*) intermingled with the brilliant blue of Cornflowers (*Centaurea cyanus*) and the white and yellows of Corn Marigolds (*Chrysanthemum segetum*), Corn Chamomile (*Anthemis arvensis*) and others. You can also include wheat and corn in the mixture.

In the first year a piece of ground should be totally cleared of all grasses and other 'weeds'. The best way is probably by a light-excluding mulch as described earlier on page 16. The soil should then be loosened and the seeds sown either in autumn or in early spring. The time of sowing will affect the flowering of the plants – an autumn sowing will flower much earlier in the year than a spring sowing.

In order to achieve stunning results in subsequent years, you will have to 'till' the soil annually, either in autumn or early spring. Do not till until all the seeds have ripened. You can either rotavate it or dig over the patch, removing any unwanted grass or 'weeds'. These cornfield flowers are not averse to growing in rich ground (in the past the fields would have been spread with 'muck' or manure), but beware: unwanted invasive plants may also appear! You will find that this kind of meadow can vary from year to year.

The pictures on these pages show the changing faces of these meadows. Most plants seem to have good and bad years, rather like the plum tree that is

overladen with fruit one year and produces nothing the next! The picture on the right is where I had rotavated part of my lawn. The flowers are in their first year and the patch was dominated by corncockles, corn chamomile and corn marigolds. Only a few poppies and cornflowers appeared – there were more in the second year.

The picture above is of another cornfield meadow, which, in that particular year, had an abundance of corn marigolds and cornflowers with a few corn chamomile – a stunning sight.

The picture on the left is of a strip of land at the edge of a farmland field of corn. It came into existence through the Entry Level Stewardship (ELS) scheme, which was launched by Defra in spring 2005. Under it, farmers will be paid for carrying out practices that would improve the environment and be beneficial to wildlife. It is a scheme that could have far-reaching consequences on our dwindling natural flora and fauna, and sights as in this picture could become common. The strip was ploughed, but then left to its own devices, but I do not know whether any flower

seeds were sown or whether they came up naturally. Poppy seeds can stay viable in the soil for many years, even centuries.

Above: Corn marigolds, cornflowers and a few corn chamomile make a stunning sight.

Left: Corncockles, corn marigolds and corn chamomile in their first year.

Right: Wood anemones and primroses often flower together in or at woodland edges.

Above: This picture is from my woodland. You could not produce foxgloves (here growing alongside a ride) in such quantity, but I cannot emphasize enough that on a smaller scale in a small garden the impact will be just as great.

Woodland meadows

The term woodland meadow is probably a figment of my imagination, since I can find no direct reference to it in any books. It probably should be called a woodland glade or a grassy ride, but meadow seems better to describe the swathes of arrestingly beautiful and breathtaking massed plants that first emerge in winter and keep going right into early summer and beyond. If you have a number of deciduous trees and shrubs, why not try to emulate, on a small scale, what occurs naturally in woods, which nature has fashioned so beautifully?

It is important that the trees or shrubs under which you establish such a meadow are deciduous, preferably native species such as Oak, Wild Cherry and Guelder Rose. It is only under deciduous trees that these plants can absorb sufficient light in the late autumn and winter to enable them to flourish. I am blessed with my own woodland, in which I can observe this wonderful procession of plants. They start to flower in January and different species emerge during the next six months. Most flowers will cease in June, but you then get graceful ferns

(some are included in the next chapter), which will adorn a woodland meadow well into late autumn.

Again, the area need not be large. Small areas in a modest-sized garden will appear proportionately large. Such a meadow also has the added advantage that most of the plants are perennials in the form of bulbs or rhizomes, which will come up and multiply year after year with very little or no maintenance. It will also provide an invaluable habitat for all kind of creatures, especially invertebrates and birds.

Depending on what you decide to plant, the first to emerge will be snowdrops and some hellebores, closely followed by wood anemones, primroses and wild daffodils. By May you should have a sea of blue in the form of bluebells. On the outer fringes you could establish foxgloves and red and white campions, which prefer more light. It does not matter that the former are biennials, because every year seedlings will appear for flowering the following season.

Other plants that will grow in these conditions include Opposite-leaved Golden Saxifrage, Townhall Clock, Herb Paris, Herb Robert, Summer Snowflake

Above: There are two wild daffodil species in Britain – *Narcissus pseudonarcissus*, shown here, and *Narcissus obvallaris*, the Tenby Daffodil. The former tend to flower a little earlier than the Tenby. The ones in the picture are in my woodland and are in only their second year, having been planted as fair-sized bulbs. In time, the clumps should increase, and, maybe if I am lucky, they will propagate themselves via seeds.

Right: Again, this picture is from my woodland. The bluebells, campions, stitchworts and yellow archangels are growing along a bank and could easily be emulated in a small garden.

and many others. Some may appear of their own accord. I would be hesitant about planting Ramsons (wild garlic) bulbs – they might just take over the whole area! Their leaves die back fairly quickly, but I have rarely seen an abundance of, say, bluebells and primroses where Ramsons are rampant. But they are a good plant to grow, so confine them to another shady spot.

The only maintenance required in such an area is keeping out unwanted plants such as brambles, or even honeysuckles and ivies, which can trail along the ground successfully vying for space and light. Moisture is important throughout the year, even during summer months. Fallen branches or prunings should not be removed, nor should any fallen leaves, in autumn. This organic 'debris' will not only feed the plants but form a natural moisture-retaining mulch. Bare soil, on the other hand, will dry out quickly during droughts and produce dust on light sandy soil and cracks in clay. Moreover, such a mulch also creates a habitat and shelter for countless beetles and other insects.

Opposite: Nature is a wonderful designer. This is a wholly natural group consisting of yellow archangel, emerging ferns, sedges and a small coppiced tree in the background. You will probably want to leave out the brambles!

Ponds, bogs and wetland meadows

In the wild there are ponds, lakes and rivers as well as marshes, bogs and fens that support a large variety of flora and fauna that would not normally be present in a conventional garden. Of course, you can hope to recreate only a microcosm of what exists in nature, but it is possible to have small areas populated with unusual plants and a myriad insects, reptiles, amphibians and other creatures.

I said at the beginning of the book that I hoped you already had a pond and that, if not, you should seriously consider building one, no matter how small. The pictures give an inkling of the effects that can be achieved. The plants growing in and around ponds are very different from those growing in bogs and fens, although some inevitably will overlap, as will the wildlife.

Gardeners and farmers spend a lot of time, care and energy making sure that their soil is well drained, since most vegetables and flowers resent being waterlogged. If you have a badly drained area, why not take advantage of it, enhance it and grow the flowers whose natural habitat is in such ground?

You may be surprised at the idea of creating a bog or fen. Nevertheless, you could make an artificial one. Dig a shallow indent about 20–25 cm deep in whatever shape you wish. Remove most of the soil and line it with a pond liner or puddling clay (the latter is preferable). Fill up with a peat substitute, leaf mould, garden compost and some of the soil (beware of invasive seeds in compost). Add water and keep topped up in very dry spells. It should be 'spongy' at all times. You now have a bog in which you can grow quite a different set of plants. Here, many of the heath family will flourish as well as Bog Asphodel (*Narthecium ossifragum*), Bog Rosemary (*Andromeda polifolia*) and Sundew (*Drosera spp.*), one of the few insectivorous plants in Britain.

The important thing about any habitat or plant is to keep on experimenting and allow at least two or three years for a plant to establish itself. If after that time it is still languishing, do not persist, but try something else.

Above: The shallow
edge of a pond
planted with
Bogbean. Here
you could also grow
Marsh Marigold,
Greater Spearwort
(*Ranunculus linqua*),
possibly
Meadowsweet,
Great Woodrush,
Water Plantain and
many others.

Left: An interesting
sight of three very
small ponds created
in a long, thin,
sloping garden. They
are entirely supplied
by rainwater off the
garage roof, diverted
from going into the
mains drain by a
simple adaptor.
Prominent in the
picture at the time
when I was there are
Wood Crane's-bill,
and in the
background Yellow
Iris and Cotton
Grass, among others.

Right: This is a little
window into a
heathland where the
heathers reign
supreme. The photo
shows Ling (*Calluna
vulgaris*). The yellow
belongs to Dwarf
Gorse (*Ulex minor*),
which is very much
smaller than the
common variety and
worth growing.
Common Gorse is
extremely good for
wildlife, but it is
large, painful and can
take over. In the
same area Bell
Heather and Cross-
leaved Heath (see
page 61) also grew in
abundance. There is
both wet and dry
heathland, but some
of the plants seem to
grow in both. The
insectivorous plants
prefer wet, and often
toads and frogs
prefer this type of
habitat rather than
sitting or swimming
in ponds, although
these are essential
for procreation.

If you have or have managed to create a 'bog', it opens up the possibility of growing a whole host of exciting and fascinating plants including carnivorous ones like Sundew (see page 59), of which there are three. Other native carnivorous species include two Butterwort and six Bladderwort. The latter normally grow submerged in water until they flower, so are better grown in a pond. However, your bog might well be suitable for the Butterwort. It would be good if you could grow any or all these insectivorous species, because they are declining not only here but throughout Europe.

If you have a lawn that remains fairly wet throughout the year, it is worth trying to establish a meadow of the rather beautiful Snake's-head Fritillaria (this plant's status as a true native is in dispute, hence the reason it is not included in the Complete List at the back of the book). In fact, you could create a 'bulbous' meadow by planting these and other spring flowering bulbs or rhizomes, including daffodils, spring squills and snowdrops, as well as autumn flowering bulbs such as autumn squills and meadow saffrons. Once the spring flowers have seeded, the lawn could be cut to make way for the autumn varieties. As with all meadows, you will have to watch out for and control overpowering grasses and other weeds, but it is a venture that could be very rewarding.

Above: A meadow of beautiful Snake's-head Fritillaria.

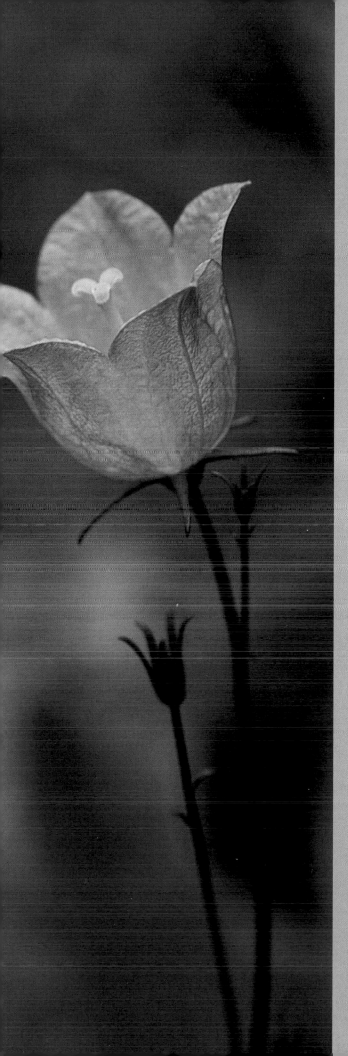

3

The Plants

EACH ENTRY IN THIS CHAPTER BEGINS
with the Latin binomial (genus and species),
followed by the popular name of the plant.
Then follows the type, the height of the plant
and its flowering season.

KEY
P *perennial* (including shrubs)
A *annual* **Bi** *biennial* **O** *orchid*

At the back of the book is a complete list of
native plants. The following pages can illustrate
only a tiny percentage of all that is available, but
I hope they give you an idea of what some look
like and a few hints on how to grow them.
Frequently I have reproduced the flowers
much larger than life, since many can easily
be overlooked and have to be examined closely
to appreciate fully their beauty and intricacies.

Achillea ptarmica Sneezewort ▲

P 90 cm *July–September*

This is a relative of the much more common Yarrow (*Achillea millefolium*) but is just as pretty and equally attractive to all kinds of insects, especially hoverflies. It flowers later in the year, so it is a good source of nectar when much else has died down. As with yarrows, there are numerous cultivars on the market, so be sure to get the original native – it is much more popular with wildlife and cultivars are contrary to the aim of this book!

Its natural habitat would be floodplain grasslands, of which there are not many left, but it also grows along roadsides near ditches, and thrives in sun or shade. The word *ptarmos* is Greek for sneezing.

Aconitum napellus Monk's Hood ▶

P 90 cm *June–September*

These handsome plants are often grown in a conventional garden border. It is unlikely they would be from true native stock, and they are grown despite the fact that they are probably one of the most poisonous plants in Britain – even just handling large bundles can cause skin irritation and palpitations. But it was also once used as a painkiller and to relieve rheumatism, and today it is still used in homeopathic medicine.

Monk's Hood seeds do not easily germinate and plants take at least two or three years to flower. It will thrive in moist soil in either full sun or light shade. Seeds and plants are widely available, but make sure they are from a native source.

Agrostemma githago Corncockle ▼

A 75 cm *June–August*

The Corncockle is not a native and does not appear in the list of plants at the end of this book. However, for centuries it used to appear, together with poppies, cornflowers, corn chamomile and others, in fields of wheat and corn that must have been colourful sights. Unfortunately, Corncockle seeds gave an unpleasant taste to bread, so, with the advent of modern technology (allowing the seeds to be separated) and extensive use of herbicides, this very pretty flower became almost extinct. Also, the fact that it will germinate only on bare and disturbed soil, and that the seeds do not remain for long in the seed bank, made its demise even more certain.

However, because it is so attractive and rare, I think it well worth cultivating in gardens. It will self-propagate if given the treatment as described under cornfield meadows (see pages 30–31).

Allium ursinum Ramsons ▲

P 60 cm *April–June*

This is yet another member of the onion family, but this time a woodland plant (also an ancient-woodland indicator), and it therefore prefers a moist, shady position. Like Chives, it readily self-seeds, likes humus-rich soil and in time forms a dense cover. However, it is active only from around December and dies down completely by midsummer, making room for other, later-flowering, plants. If you can find a wood where it is present, you will have no trouble collecting seeds, since it normally grows in abundance. Remember that seeds have to be harvested in early summer.

Ramsons are also known as Wild Garlic. All parts are edible and can be used in the same way as conventional garlic. In fact, its health and medicinal properties are greater than those of the conventional garlic cloves.

Anacamptis pyramidalis Pyramidal Orchid ▼

O 60 cm *June–August*

Today, no orchid can be called common or widespread, although this one is found more frequently than most. It grows throughout the UK, but the majority are found in the south of England on calcareous soils. Once established on ground that suits them, they can spread rapidly. The one in the picture was a solitary specimen found by a roadside ditch in Sussex (a bit past its sell-by flowering date!), despite the fact it prefers to grow among grasses in dry sunny places.

Plugs of this orchid can be purchased, and I would advise planting them on neutral or slightly alkaline soil, and, if possible, on soil containing lime. If you are lucky, they (or it) may spread. Never transplant an orchid – it will end in grief. Cherish it and grow with it some tall grasses such as Erect Brome (*Bromus erectus*). Insects are attracted to all orchids.

If you find this orchid in the wild, you can collect seeds in early to mid-August and try your hand at growing it yourself (see page 22).

Althaea officinalis Marsh Mallow ▲

P 2 m *August–September*

Some years ago, I bought a single potted specimen of this rather handsome plant in the hope that I might one day attempt to make marsh mallows from its roots (it was once used to make these sweets). I never got round to it, nor did I expect it to do well, since its natural habitat is in brackish water by the sea. All it got was my heavy clay. Nevertheless, it thrived, and today I have a job keeping it under control – old plants develop great, thick, woody roots, and self-seeded new ones appear in profusion every year.

It is probably easier to buy a single plant, unless you want an immediate 'big show'. If you obtain seeds, they should be sown direct into the ground in autumn so the hard seeds can take advantage of winter frosts.

Andromeda polifolia Bog-rosemary ▼

P 35 cm *May–September*

This would be a very good plant to grow in your bog (see page 36) – that is, if you are going to create one. Another good candidate would be the Bog Pimpernel illustrated on the left. It will also grow in normal, damp soil. Bog-rosemary is now quite rare and a very pretty, shrubby plant well worth growing in the garden.

Anagallis arvensis Scarlet Pimpernel ▲

A 10 cm *May–October*

Long before this charming plant sprang into fame through Baroness Orczy's Scarlet Pimpernel novels, it was known as the Poor Man's Weatherglass or Shepherd's Clock, since the petals open at 8 a.m., close at 2 p.m. and do not open at all in bad weather.

Scarlet Pimpernel are widespread and can be found throughout the British Isles on open sunny ground. Its cousin, the Yellow Pimpernel (*Lysimachia nemorum*), is a woodland plant and prefers shade and moisture.

It has another cousin, the Bog Pimpernel (*Anagallis palustris*), illustrated below. This is not as common and is usually found only in wet, marshy conditions – a good candidate for your homemade bog. It has lovely pink flowers that are slightly scented.

Anemone nemorosa Wood Anemone ▼

P 30 cm *March–May*

The Wood Anemone and the Bluebell must be one of the glories of ancient woodlands in the UK. Wood Anemones form breathtaking carpets of white (sometimes flushed pink) in early spring. They appear quickly (unlike the Bluebell, which can start pushing up its leaves at Christmas), and, almost as quickly, all signs of them, even leaves, disappear, leaving the ground free for other plants.

Wood Anemone does not often form fertile seed, but spreads through creeping rhizomes at an agonisingly slow pace – only a metre or so every hundred years! You will, therefore, probably have to buy plugs or pot plants and put them under deciduous shrubs. Do not plant them under evergreens, because they require winter light and sunshine to stimulate growth.

Angelica sylvestris Wild Angelica ▲

P 90 cm *July–August*

This is a tall stately plant with a thick hollow stem that normally grows in damp meadows and woods. Unlike its foreign cousin, *A. archangelica*, which is much used for culinary purposes, this one is not good to eat, but a great favourite of all kinds of wildlife. You can find its domed white flower heads awash with hoverflies, bees and many other insects. Try to resist cutting off the seed stems, even if they look untidy, since birds will appreciate them. It is very easy to grow either from seed or potted plants, and can spread quite rapidly, provided it gets sufficient moisture.

Anthyllis vulneraria Kidney Vetch ▲

P 60 cm *June–September*

Kidney Vetch is the source of food for the Small Blue butterfly, and for that reason alone it should be worth growing. Apart from that, it is a very hardy colourful plant that will probably establish itself anywhere. It will grow best in very well drained light soils.

Aquilegia vulgaris Columbine ▼

P 90 cm *May–July*

There are numerous cultivars of all hues and colour combinations of this popular plant, but the true native is normally only blue/purple. It is scarce and grows in fens, woods and waste ground. I have blue ones scattered all over the garden, but it seems unlikely they are true wild specimens. Botanists often refer to plants as 'garden escapes' and therefore not true natives. I am sure their scarcity is due not only to loss of habitat but also to the days when people avidly picked and dug up wild flowers because they were exceptionally pretty, and thought they would look well in the garden.

Columbines are easily grown from seed, and existing plants will readily seed themselves.

Arum italicum ssp. neglectum
Italian Lords-and-Ladies ▼
P 60 cm *May–June*

Arum maculatum Lords-and-Ladies
P 30 cm *April–May*

Both these plants are similar and normally grow in woodlands, preferring shade and moist soils. Once established, they are liable to appear anywhere, like the one illustrated growing tight against the brick wall of my house facing south in bright sun!

The leaves of *A. maculatum* are often spotted and the long spadix is normally brown, whereas in *A. italicum ssp. neglectum* it is wholly green/yellow and the leaves are never spotted.

Both have bright-red berries in autumn, which are poisonous to humans and not all that palatable to wildlife. In hard winters, thrushes may scratch up the roots, and pheasants have been known to eat the berries. In fact, this may be a case of fauna being beneficial to flora: the flowers, both male and female, are inside the spathe (not visible) and exude an irresistible scent that lures insects inside to pollinate the female flowers at the bottom. Since there are also downward-facing hairs inside, the insect is sometimes trapped inside where it remains doomed!

Seeds are easy to find in hedgerows and you should have no problems germinating them.

Armeria maritima Thrift ▲

P 30 cm *April–August*

Often found in rockeries in conventional gardens, this pretty plant forms soft cushions with pink (sometimes white) flowers. It is well worth growing, since it flowers from spring to autumn. The leaves are very narrow and form a dense mass in order to better conserve water. Although it originates all along the coasts of England on cliffs and in salt marshes, it nevertheless grows easily in almost any garden soils.

Asplenium trichomanes
Maidenhair Spleenwort ▼

P 20 cm *May–October*

This is a lovely little fern that remains bright and cheerful all
year. It is ideally suited to crevices in walls or any small
spaces in rockeries, and once established seems to require
very little attention.

Astragalus danicus **Purple Milk-vetch** ▶

P 30 cm *May–July*

Neither this nor the other plant below from the same family
is very common. This one is a small perennial that grows
mainly on the eastern side of England and Scotland in
grassland meadows, so many of which have now been lost. It
would be a good perennial species to include if you are
planning a grassland meadow patch. If not, try to plant it in
well-drained soil, preferably calcareous.

Purple Milk-vetch (it is normally not as red as it appears
in the picture) is on the most recent Red Data List of
vulnerable British plants (May 2005) and is listed as
endangered.

Astragalus glycyphyllos **Wild Liquorice** ◀

P 90 cm *June–August*

Unlike Purple Milk-vetch, this plant, also called plain Milk-
vetch, grows only in central and the southeastern half of
England – rarely in the north – and is totally absent from
Ireland. It too prefers chalky soil, and the specimen in the
photograph was sprawling horizontally along a roadside
hedge.

Both plants have the very distinctive pinnate leaves of
the pea family. I assume it gets the name 'Wild Liquorice'
from the taste of the roots, which used to be chewed by
children in Victorian times. There are numerous species of
Astragalus in the world, many of which are used in
alternative medicine, and are also grown as cattle feed.
They are attractive to many insects.

Athyrium filix-femina Lady-fern ▼

P 1.5 m *July–August*

Ferns are attractive anywhere, but this delicate and stunning native is a must if you are going to grow any ferns at all in your garden. Even before it comes into full leaf, the unfurling fronds are truly elegant. Like all ferns, it requires shade and moisture all the year. The spores (seeds) appear on the underside of the leaves in autumn, but I would advise trying to obtain a pot plant. Collecting the dustlike spores is rather like trying to collect fungi spores, and getting them to germinate can be tricky and frustrating.

Atropa belladonna Deadly Nightshade ▼

P 1.5 m *June–August*

I have included this unusual climber mainly to enable you to distinguish it from Black (or Woody) Nightshade and Bittersweet. The latter pair both grow in my garden and visitors often think they are the poisonous Deadly Nightshade. In fact, neither is poisonous, although both could give you a bad stomach ache. However, all parts of Deadly Nightshade are very poisonous, the root more so than the black berries (sometimes called devil's or witch's berries), which ripen in autumn. Despite all its deadly notoriety, the plant is also widely used in medicine.

Blechnum spicant Hard Fern ▼

P 70 cm *August–November*

This is a true woodland fern, requiring moisture and shade. I have it in my wood, where it sometimes dies down in winter, re-emerging in spring with lovely fresh, green, unfurling fronds that can light up the darkness of a woodland floor.

Hard Fern prefers neutral to acid soils, and plants are easy to buy. Growing from spores can by tricky, but do try it if you feel adventurous. Make sure that the spores stay on top of the soil and that they never dry out.

Butomus umbellatus Flowering-rush ▼

P 1 m *July–August*

Despite its name, this does not belong to the rush family. It doubtless gets its name from the way the flowers grow, which is similar to many rushes. It is an ideal plant for a small pond. It is not invasive and can be left for several years, after which the plant should be divided. It will also grow in slow-moving water.

Briza media Quaking-grass ▼

P 50 cm *June–August*

This is a real 'fun' grass, attractive both in spring and late summer, when it produces its rustling, straw-coloured seed heads, from which is gets its name. The photograph shows it in spring with pretty purple-headed buds. It is a perennial, easy to grow in full sun, but beware: it can self-seed everywhere! I visited one lady's garden in which it had seeded wherever it could find a sunny spot – between paving stones, beds and borders.

Caltha palustris Marsh-marigold ▼

P 30 cm *March–August*

If you already have a pond in your garden, you will find that Marsh-marigolds are good marginal plants. They will also grow in shallow moving water, or any wet boggy place. Marsh-marigolds can have a long flowering season (I have had some come into bloom in February), but they are at their best in April and May. They also develop into magnificently large clumps, some 40–50 cm across, which can be split.

Campanula latifolia Giant Bellflower ▼

P 90 cm *July–September*

This is a tall handsome plant that would grace any border that has some shade. In garden conditions with no competitors it could grow over one metre tall. Its natural habitat is wood and hedgerows like its similar cousin the Nettle-leaved Bellflower (*Campanula trachelium*). I once tried growing the latter from seed, and although I had no problem in germinating them and potting them on till they were sizable plants, once I planted them out not one survived! The culprits were rabbits who totally razed them to below the crowns!

Unless you live in the heart of the country, rabbits should not be a problem, but slugs could be since they seem particularly partial to bellflowers. If so, use a slug deterrent such as grit, or even lure them to an inebriated death with beer traps sunk into the ground.

Campanula glomerata Clustered Bellflower ▲

P 60 cm *June–August*

Both these members of the Bellflower family are handsome species, which is no doubt why there are literally dozens of cultivars and hybrids available from nurseries. It may be tempting to buy some of these, but do try to keep to the true native species, which will have a far greater effect on the wildlife in your garden. This and the the Nettle-leaved Bellflower would make good bedfellows in the garden as they require similar conditions.

Campanula rotundifolia Harebell ▶

P 60 cm *July–September*

The dainty Harebell was voted the official flower of Co. Antrim, where they aptly also call it Witches', Goblins' or Puck's Thimble. In Scotland it is often called the Scottish Bluebell.

The seeds are minute and should be sown in autumn. If you would rather sow in spring, they ought to undergo cold stratification. Otherwise, buy a few plants and occasionally divide them in autumn or spring. Harebells attract many insects, and it is the main food plant of the Ingrailed Clay Moth.

Carlina vulgaris Carline Thistle ◀

<u>Bi</u> 30 cm *July–September*

Unlike other thistles, the flower of this one is not pinkish/purple, but is straw-coloured and looks as if it has dried out. This may be the case, because it retains the same look for many months rather like an everlasting flower. The plant has only one stem, which often bears only a single flower. It is infrequent but usually found on dry chalky land and has the distinction of being the food source for the not-exactly-attractive larvae of the Metzneria aestivelle moth.

Cichorium intybus Chicory ▼

<u>P</u> 1 m *July–October*

The word chicory (sometimes called Succory) will conjure up in many people's minds either 'coffee' made from the bitter roasted roots or winter vegetables, including the brightly coloured radicchio. But there is also a wild native Chicory, quite tall, with brilliant blue flowers well worth cultivating in the garden. A very good plant for bees, but it also houses countless other insects.

Cardamine pratensis Cuckooflower ▲

<u>P</u> 60 cm *April–June*

Very little needs to be said about this common but dainty and charming lilac-pink flower. You do not often see them massed, as in the photograph, but this is, I think, the way you should grow them. I found this clump in a hedgerow near a ditch, where it had all the right conditions: part sun and moisture. Grow it with other spring flowers (I had some growing with Cowslips in the foreground, which looked stunning, flowering at the same time) or make it part of a woodland or grassland meadow – it is very accommodating! It is also a favourite food for the caterpillars of the Orange Tip and Green-veined White Butterfly.

Circaea lutetiana Enchanter's Nightshade ▲

P 60 cm *June–August*

This plant is really enchanting and can light up a shady place on dusky evenings. It spreads readily through rhizomes. The Elephant Hawk-moth caterpillar feeds on this plant. The name comes from the sorceress Circe who turned Ulysses' shipmates into pigs!

Cirsium palustre Marsh Thistle ▶

Bi 1.3 m *July–September*

Thistles may not be everyone's idea of a plant in the garden, but as far as birds, especially finches, are concerned you could have nothing better. The Marsh Thistle is one of the tallest and, of course, prefers damp places, whereas the Dwarf Thistle is the smallest and prefers dry soil. The latter has one stemless, solitary flower per plant.

Clematis vitalba Traveller's-joy ▶

<u>P</u> 30 cm *July–September*

Among its many other names, this climber is also called Old
Man's Beard (from the fluffy, feathery seeds) and really
needs very little introduction, since it is common in
hedgerows throughout the country. It is also a great
provider to wildlife: many moth larvae feed on it, bees and
hoverflies love its nectar and the seeds are food for many
birds and small mammals in winter.

In the garden you can either let it 'roam' wild or cut it
back hard in winter. If there is nothing up which it can
climb, it will also trail along the ground. Like the cultivated
clematis, it prefers its roots in the shade in a nonacidic soil.

Colchicum autumnale
Meadow Saffron/Autumn Crocus ◀

<u>P</u> 30 cm *August–September*

This pretty mauve plant causes endless confusion –
including to me! It has nothing to do with the crocuses that
come out in spring, nor should it be confused with the plant
from whose stamens saffron is produced – all of which are
called crocuses! It belongs to the *Colchicum* species (part of
the Lily group), of which there are many all flowering in
autumn, but *C. autumnale* is the only native.

It grows mainly in eastern Wales, Dorset and the
Midlands. One can purchase seeds and corms, which should
be planted in late summer in shade and humus-rich soil.
Plant the corms at least 8 cm deep, at which depth there is
less chance that mice and other rodents will get to them.
It flowers in autumn and produces abundant glossy leaves
in spring.

Convallaria majalis Lily-of-the-valley ▼

P 30 cm *May–June*

The charming, nodding, fragrant bell-like flowers make Lily-of-the-valley one of the most popular and beautiful of British wild plants. In my experience, it seems to grow best in damp shade, but elsewhere I have seen it grow in almost full sun. On the other hand, some books will tell you it grows on calcareous, dry soil in woods! Once well established, the rhizomes of large clumps can be split up into many individuals: bear in mind each plant has only two leaves to a single flower stem.

Bees love the flowers, and I can imagine birds and small mammals making use of the red berries.

Cornus suecica Dwarf Cornel ▼

P 30 cm *July–September*

This is a species under threat in the UK. At present it can be found only in the north of England, but more frequently in Scotland. Since the red berries are also a winter food for the Inuit, climate change could also threaten it, since it obviously grows in far colder climes than the UK can offer. The red berries must also be a welcome food for birds in the snow.

Crithmum maritimum Rock Samphire ▲

P 40 cm *June–October*

Although this is a yellow umbellifer from the carrot family, its fleshy leaves can deceive you into thinking it is a succulent. It grows largely in stabilized shingle and on cliffs round the coasts of Britain, but I am sure it can adapt to garden conditions.

In 1824, an adventurous plant collector, the Rev. Leonard Jenyn wrote, '*The green succulent stalks of this plant are in great request for pickling, and hence arises another cause of its scarcity; since wherever it can be got at, it is seldom suffered to remain long by the poor people, who greedily gather it for this purpose.*'

It is not very common today, possibly because of overcollecting in the past.

Cynoglossum officinale **Hound's-tongue** ▼

Bi 60 cm *May–August*

This tall plant with relatively small flowers is very popular
with insects but unpalatable to livestock, and for this reason
seems to have been almost 'hounded' out of existence. This
is not the reason why it is called 'Hound's-tongue':
apparently, if you put a leaf under each foot in your shoe,
this should stop dogs barking at you, in other words 'tie the
hound's tongue'. It has another curiosity: it does not have a
particularly pleasant odour, hence the old English name
'Rats and Mice'. Nevertheless, it is a handsome plant, but I
would not put it into any kind of meadow, because it can
spread and could overpower most other meadow species.
Make sure you put it in full sun, preferably in light soil.

Cuscuta epithymum **Dodder** ▲

A 1 m *June–October*

If you are after something exotic and dramatic, even a bit
horrific, why not try your hand at growing Dodder, which
also happens to be on the Red Data list? It is not, however,
on Schedule 8 of the Countryside Act. Because it is a true
parasite, you first have to have some host plants that you do
not mind being engulfed or even devoured, because Dodder
will suck all their moisture and nutrients. These include
gorse, thyme and heathers. Also, I am not sure that you can
even buy any seeds (you certainly cannot buy plants), so you
will have to search for some yourself. If you are lucky you
will find Dodder growing on heaths and the seeds ripen in
autumn. Be very careful collecting seeds, and take some only
if there are plenty. These should immediately be scattered on
and around the stems of the chosen host plants. With luck,
they will germinate the following season.

No part of Dodder is ever green, since it does not
produce chlorophyll – the stems are red and twine
themselves round the host plants (similar to bindweed – it
belongs to the same family) and eventually produces a
sweet-smelling, pinkish white flower.

Dactylorhiza fuchsii
Common Spotted-orchid ◄

O 45 cm *June–August*

These three orchids are part of the *Dactylorhiza* group and should not present too many problems in growing. The top picture is a close-up of the Common Spotted displaying all its exquisite orderly detail. I have it growing all over my garden and woods. Some were always present, but they self-seeded rapidly wherever undergrowth was cleared and they had sufficient light. You can now purchase seed of this species. I am sure you will have a good chance of succeeding with them if you sow the seeds in a light place among meadow grasses or among other plants.

The Northern Marsh-orchid grows in the north of England and Wales, but is rare elsewhere. It can be found in fens and some meadows. The Southern Marsh-orchid is fairly common in Wales and the Southern half of England and grows in damp meadows.

Dactylorhiza praetermissa
Southern Marsh-orchid ▼

O 60 cm *June–July*

Dactylorhiza purpurella
Northern Marsh-orchid ▼

O 30 cm *June–July*

Deschampsia flexuosa Wavy Hair-grass ▲

P 2 m *June–July*

I have tried many times, without success, to do photographic justice to this grass. It is very beautiful and I would have it even as a pot plant. It can be grown on its own or among other plants, but it is also ideal in a grassland meadow. The flowering stems come out of tight mounds of deep-green leaves. The buds are silky and wavy, and the flowers become bright pinpricks in sunlight.

Dianthus gratianopolitanus Cheddar Pink ▼

P 30 cm *May–July*

Dianthus deltoides Maiden Pink ▼

P 60 cm *June–September*

There must be literally hundreds of pinks available from garden centres, but there are only three native species: these two, and the Deptford Pink (*D. armeria*). All three are on the Red Data List as endangered, threatened or very vulnerable. This is a great pity, since they are beautiful little plants and wonderful to see growing wild. The first is natural only to the Cheddar Gorge, while the Maiden Pink grows in the southern half of England, as does the Deptford Pink. Do not collect seeds, but try to buy some from a reputable source.

All pinks like to grow in full sun and well-drained soil and clumps should spread once well established. The scent of the flowers seems to attract many insects to feed on the nectar.

Dipsacus fullonum Wild Teasel ▶

Bi 2 m *July–August*

Teasel are tall architectural-looking plants (until the wind blows them over!), and are good for wildlife in the garden, especially birds. There were no Wild Teasels in my area, so some years ago I sowed some, which flowered, and then nothing happened for several years. I began to think that the birds had devoured all the seeds (finches swinging on flowerheads are a great sight), when suddenly they reappeared and are now growing everywhere! So beware.

Drosera rotundifolia Round-leaved Sundew ▼

P 10 cm *June–August*

If you have managed to establish your own peaty bog in the garden, this is the place to grow Sundews. They are interesting plants, becoming increasingly rare due to habitat loss, and one of the few native insectivorous species. In the sun their leaf tips appear to sparkle with tiny dewdrops (hence the name), which are in fact a gluelike substance that entraps small insects. Maybe not exactly the plant to encourage fauna, but at least they may reduce the population of midges and the like that have been spawned in your bog!

Seeds are minute, but plants can be purchased. Seedlings will have to be fed small insects, not compost!

Dryas octopetala Mountain Avens ▼

P 6 cm *May–July*

A lovely shrubby plant with pure white, roselike flowers (it belongs to that family), which is very suitable for a sunny rockery or where ground cover is required. Sow seed in late summer. You can also easily propagate the plant either by cuttings or layering, also in late summer. It has two cousins, Wood and Water Avens, but they are not as attractive as this one.

Epipactis helleborine Broad-leaved Helleborine ◄

O 90 cm *July–September*

I have a few of these Helleborines in my woods. But they are very erratic in their appearance – it seems they can stay dormant in the ground for many years and then suddenly make a dramatic appearance, presumably when all the conditions are to their liking.

The species prefers part shade and often grows among native trees such as oak and beech.

Epipactis palustris *Marsh Helleborine* ▼

O 60 cm *July–August*

If you can successfully introduce one or two plants into the garden, it can be very rewarding, because, in the right conditions, they can spread and produce a wonderful show in late summer. They require a wet, sunny area, and should be planted in calcareous soil. On no account use any artificial fertilizers, or indeed any chemicals. The best time to plant is late autumn.

Echium vulgare Viper's-bugloss ▼

Bi 60 cm *June–September*

A handsome, useful biennial with lovely bright-blue flowers and pink buds that prefers chalk and limestone in the wild but will grow anywhere if nurtured. It is often grown by organic vegetable gardeners as it attracts a host of bees as well as other insects, including hoverflies, which are predators of aphids.

Erica cinerea Bell Heather ▲

P 75 cm *July–September*

Erica tetralix Cross-leaved Heath ▶

P 70 cm *June–October*

These two plants, together with Ling (*Calluna vulgaris*), grow in abundance on heathland and drier bogs. Unfortunately, these habitats are not only rare, but where there are still heaths much is being overrun by invasive plants such as Bracken and alien Rhododendron. Despite preferring acid soils, they will grow almost anywhere, including my garden.

Cross-leaved Heath, so called because of the way the leaves grow, actually has larger flowers than Bell Heather, but is considerably paler, and both would make a good mixture anywhere where low, bushy plants are appropriate. Bees, of course, love all heathers, but the leaves and stems contain many chemicals that make them indigestible to browsing animals.

Euphrasia officinalis agg. Eyebright ▼

A 25 cm *July–September*

There are several hundred species of this plant in the world and two or three dozen in Britain. In books it is often listed as 'agg.' (aggregate), since many of the British species are very localized and difficult to tell apart.

I have large numbers of these plants growing in the grass of some woodland rides. They look like speckled cushions amid the green, and it is not until one looks at them closely that they reveal an extremely pretty but tiny flower only a few millimetres wide.

I have never tried establishing them in the garden, but I have no doubt they would fill up spaces in 'meadows' if given good sun and reasonable moisture. They are partially parasites of grass and other plants, so would not do well on their own.

Eupatorium cannabinum Hemp-agrimony ▲

P 90 cm *July–September*

Hemp Agrimony is a tall, robust plant that could get out of hand if not watched closely, because it self-seeds profusely. It is widespread and can be found in a variety of habitats, although on the whole it prefers damp situations and will tolerate full sun or shade. The large, pinkish white, flat flower heads that have earned it the name 'raspberries and cream' (I think it looks more like a long-haired rug) seem to act like a magnet to all kinds of insects. Many butterflies and moths feed on the nectar.

Filipendula ulmaria Meadowsweet ▶

P 1.5 m *June–September*

Filipendula vulgaris Dropwort ▼

P 90 cm *June–September*

Both plants produce a lovely show of white flowers, are very easy to grow and are complementary. If your garden is on the dry side, grow Dropwort, which has pretty leaves staying near the ground with the flowers on a tall stem. Meadowsweet is much more robust, has a good show of pinnate leaves and prefers wet soil. The flowers are also slightly scented.

Both plants are attractive to insects and beetles and are easy to grow either from seed or purchased plants. Make sure Dropwort is planted in full sun.

Galanthus nivalis Snowdrop ▼

P 30 cm *January–March*

No garden is really complete without this delicate, now nearly Christmas-flowering, plant. Seed is not very viable, so propagate by bulb division. Plant bulbs to a depth of 8–10 cm in autumn in dappled shade and a moist position.

Galium odoratum Woodruff ▶

P 30 cm *May–June*

Many of the Bedstraw family can be a bit of a nuisance, especially in early autumn, when their seeds and stems seem to cling to everything, especially my large long-haired dog! However, all of them are very good for wildlife, and seeds of this one are not quite as bad as some.

The picture shows Sweet Woodruff growing in a garden, and, massed in a bed, they give off a wonderful aroma.

Genista tinctoria Dyer's Greenweed ▲

P 1.5 m *July–September*

As its names implies, this low-growing evergreen shrub is used by dyers for obtaining various shades of yellow. I do not think you will have any problems growing it – one plant is probably enough to start with. It will spread rapidly and if not watched it may take over. It will grow on any soil but prefers heavy clay. Also, the soil should not be too rich, because it may then flower only sparsely.

It is the favourite flood plant of the beautiful Green Hairstreak butterfly. It will lay its eggs on the leaves that then feed the larvae.

Gentianella campestris Field Gentian ▶

Bi 30 cm *June–September*

This small, pretty member of the Gentian family, so reluctant to open its flowers except in full sunshine, is now on the Red Data List. It grows in the north of England, Scotland and parts of Ireland, mostly on neutral grasslands. It is well worth growing in the garden – that is if you can purchase seeds or plants.

Geranium pratense Meadow Crane's-bill ▲

P 90 cm *June–September*

Geranium sanguineum Bloody Crane's-bill ▶

P 60 cm *July–August*

There must be literally hundreds of Geranium species, cultivars and hybrids in the world, and there are no fewer than twelve native species. All of them are worth bringing into the garden, but my favourite has to be Meadow Crane's-bill. It is just beautiful in its captivating blue, either growing on its own or in a grassland meadow. The same applies to the vivid Bloody Crane's-bill.

Wood Crane's-bill prefers a little more shade as well as damp. All three benefit from having dead flower heads and leaves removed to prolong the flowering season. You may find the seeds tricky to germinate, but pot plants are widely available.

Geranium sylvaticum Wood Crane's-bill ▶

P 60 cm *June–July*

Geum rivale Water Avens ▲

P 60 cm *April–September*

Water Avens have a long flowering season and are well worth establishing if you have somewhere permanently wet, or around a pond. If you have any problem keeping the soil damp enough, mulch well with plenty of organic matter. At the time of writing, I sowed some seeds, but I have many of its cousin, Herb Bennet (*Geum urbanum*), with which it apparently hybridizes liberally. I have no idea what the offspring look like, but I am sure some are available in garden centres.

Water Avens spreads underground, sending up new plantlets, which can be dug up and planted elsewhere.

Glaucium flavum Yellow Horned-poppy ▶

Bi 90 cm *June–September*

This is the poppy that I tried, unsuccessfully, to germinate (see page 20), but I have not given up hope: it may well spring up in the future. However, my soil is not ideal, since it is a coastal plant, often growing on shingle just above the tide mark.

Gymnadenia conopsea Fragrant Orchid ▲

O 60 cm *June–July*

Fragrant Orchids thrive best on unimproved calcareous grassland. The most famous sites are probably Salisbury Plain and Porton Down. Both have been designated as Special Areas of Conservation (SACs) under European legislation. The orchid will, however, grow in many other habitats. The flowers are usually pink, lilac or rosy-purple in colour, but specimens with white flowers have also been found. It has a very powerful scent. All orchids do, of course, attract countless insects – they make quite sure by various and

devious means that their flowers are pollinated. Apparently, Charles Darwin 'caught a moth sucking at this orchid with a pollen-mass of *Habenaria bifolia* sticking to it'. *Habenaria bifolia* or *Platanthera bifolia* is the Lesser Butterfly Orchid.

Hedera helix Ivy ▼

P 30 m *September–November*

Ivy is one of the most important plants for wildlife, so do try to find a place for at least one specimen to grow – up your house, fence or a large tree. You may think that Ivy will eventually damage a tree but this is not so: a healthy tree will cohabit quite happily. It is also important that you get the ivy into its adult stage (which may take a few years), when it will flower and bear fruit. It requires some sunlight to get to this stage.

Ivy flowers in autumn/early winter and is a great source of nectar to all insects when little else is available. The fruits appear in the new year and are an important source of food for all birds, including the newly arrived migrants – again, when not much else is around. In addition, is offers shelter to many: birds will nest in mature specimens and bats find it a useful shelter and even use it as a roosting site.

Helianthemum nummularium Common Rock-rose ▲

P 30 cm *June–September*

Anyone with a rockery almost certainly has some Helianthemums, but they are probably one of the numerous cultivars, hybrids and imports. If so, do replace them with this lovely native variety that is food for so many butterflies. Although insects are attracted to the various varieties, none are as good as the native species. I would advise initially buying a plant or two and then propagating from cuttings taken in summer, since the seeds can sometimes be tricky.

Remarkably, this plant feeds the larva of the Brown Argus, Green Hairstreak, Northern Brown Argus and Silver-studded Blue.

Heracleum sphondylium Hogweed ▼

<u>Bi/P</u> 2.5 m *April–September*

Hogweed is similar to its umbellifer cousin, Angelica, but will grow in drier conditions. Unfortunately, it is also much more persistent and can become a nuisance and very difficult to dig out once established. However, it also acts as an absolute magnet to all kinds of insects. Normally, insects fly off immediately you come close with a camera (trying to get them to stay is a lengthy business), but not so with Hogweed. Perhaps some of its essential oils and ingredients are irresistible and addictive! The plant is used in herbal medicine.

Himantoglossum hircinum Lizard Orchid ▶

<u>O</u> 90 cm *June–July*

A fantastic orchid with a haunting beauty all its own. It is rare and unpredictable in its appearance, and England is on the northernmost fringes of its habitat (it grows throughout much of southern Europe). The largest colonies are in Kent, where it grows on calcareous grasslands. You must not collect seed of this orchid, and, if buying plants, make sure they are from a really reputable source.

Helleborus foetidus Stinking Hellebore ▲

<u>P</u> 80 cm *January–May*

This plant does not 'stink'. In fact, it has quite a pleasant odour until you crush the leaves, when the smell is unpleasant and can cause irritation to your hands. No part of it should be ingested, since it is poisonous.

It is a good perennial that will grow in almost any soil, in shade or sunlight, and has the added advantage that it comes into flower as early as January. It prefers really damp places, so, unless you have somewhere suitable, it will probably be best grown in shade. It does well with rich organic matter added, and, once established, it resents being transplanted. It will spread by underground rhizomes.

The plant is quite rare, so it may be difficult to obtain seeds, but plants are sold in pots and plugs. Make sure you get the native species and not one of the many garden cultivars. Note the hibernating Ladybird, of which there were many when I photographed it.

Hippocrepis comosa Horseshoe Vetch ◄

P 10 cm *April–July*

If you drive along the South Downs coast road in spring, you may see banks on the north side smothered in yellow flowers. These will probably be the Horseshoe Vetch. Very poor chalk grasslands are its natural habitat – the poorer the better, because it will keep out any competition. The reason it survives in extreme and poor conditions is that this plant has its own source of nitrogen in the form of nodules on the roots. This is also true of many of the huge pea family, including garden vegetables – namely peas and beans.

I think it will do well in almost any soil in the garden as long as you keep competition from other plants to a minimum. The seeds are said to have a poor germination rate, so maybe it would be wise to purchase plants.

It is an extremely important plant for butterflies and their larvae: it is the major and sometimes only source of food for the Adonis Blue, Chalkhill Blue, Berger's Clouded Yellow, Silver-studded Blue and Dingy Skipper.

Hyacinthoides non-scripta Bluebell ►

P 30 cm *April–June*

The Bluebell is often referred to as a British phenomenon, despite the fact that it grows in a number of other European countries. Nevertheless, it attracts many coachloads of visitors in spring (including from abroad) because nowhere else can one see such an astonishing haze of blue created by a single plant species.

The Bluebell's natural home is ancient woodlands, from which it travels only slowly and shyly. It can be seen in many hedgerows, ditches and even fields, but these are only indicators that once these too were covered in forests full of flowers. Despite its numbers, the Bluebell is also under threat: until quite recently it suffered wholesale digging up, some by commercial organizations, and its 'purity' is now threatened by the sale and planting of the more robust Spanish Bluebell, which is often sold under ambiguous labels in garden centres and superstores. Some also believe that climate warming will drive it northwards, but I believe that severe droughts, of which there will be more in future, could also have drastic effects.

Genuine Bluebell seeds can easily be collected, and bulbs raised from the true plants can be purchased. If you decide to grow from seed, just make sure the soil never dries out and be prepared to wait for two to four years before the plantlets will flower. Strictly speaking, you require a permit to collect these seeds but this is to prevent wholesale exploitation (bulldozers have been used to dig up bulbs), and I doubt whether you would be prosecuted for collecting a few seeds for the garden!

Hypericum androsaemum Tutsan ▲

P 70 cm *June–August*

All the Hypericums are good plants for wildlife, and this is a delightful little shrub that has bright yellow flowers followed by black and red berries, which give it interest over a long period. Once you have one plant established, it will self-seed readily. One appeared out of nowhere in my vegetable garden and now there is quite a collection.

Iris pseudacorus Yellow Iris ▶

P 90 cm *June–August*

Yellow Iris is often thought of as a pond plant. This is so, but it will grow equally well in soil where it is damp all year. It is a very handsome plant with its tall swordlike leaves and fluttering bright flowers, and is also known as Yellow Flag.

Kickxia spuria **Round-leaved Fluellen** ▲

A 30 cm *July–October*

This is now a rarity, probably because it is one of the arable plants that used to appear in cornfields. It is well worth cultivating, especially in a meadow (see page 30–31).

Knautia arvensis **Field Scabious** ▶

P/Bi 90 cm *July–September*

Field Scabious is not only very pretty and easy to grow, but is also a very important plant for butterflies and others. It is one of the food plants for the Marsh Fritillary larvae and the White Letter Hairstreak, and a source of nectar to many others, including bees and other insects. The size and colour can vary considerably depending on soil. Its natural habitat is chalky downlands, but it will probably grow almost anywhere. It is also aptly called Lady's Pincushion or Blue Bonnets.

Lamium album White Dead-nettle ▲

<u>P</u> 60 cm *April–November*

Lamiastrum galeobdolon Yellow Archangel ▲

<u>P</u> 60 cm *April–July*

Lamium purpureum Red Dead-nettle ▶

<u>A</u> 30 cm *March–December*

On this page are three members of the very large Labiate family, which also includes mints, thymes and hemp-nettles. They are all very attractive to insects and most have gaping mouths and little platforms on which insects can alight. The Yellow Archangel is a wondrous plant when viewed closely and is good for woodland edges. The Red and White Dead-nettle are very common but can make good, long-lasting ground cover, especially the former, when in full sun.

Lathyrus sylvestris ▲
Narrow-leaved Everlasting-pea

<u>P</u> 2 m *June–August*

This is a very pretty scrambling plant that you could put in a hedge or let climb over a trellis. As its species name, *sylvestris*, implies, it is a woodland plant and found on woodland verges, but is now relatively rare in the wild, so well worth cultivating. It is faintly scented and therefore has a special attraction for moths flying at night. It is also the food plant of the Long-tailed Blue, a rare migrant to Britain, which breeds here occasionally – it seems our climate is too cold – something that may change in future.

Lavatera arborea Tree-mallow ▲

<u>Bi</u> 3 m *June–September*

Unfortunately, this lovely tall plant is a biennial, although it looks much more like a perennial. You therefore have to ensure that there is always a succession of plants coming up with the ones that are flowering. Once they are established,

I am sure you will find seedlings coming up of their own accord, but you must remember that its natural home is along the south and west coasts of England. It is therefore important that you find a spot that it likes, or alternatively collect seeds and sow them in boxes every year. It is one of the plants I sowed as an experiment (see page 20–21) and the germination rate was not very high. On the other hand, you need only a few plants for a spectacular show.

Leucojum aestivum Summer Snowflake ▼

<u>P</u> 60 cm *April–June*

Regrettably, I was unable to get to either Wiltshire or Berkshire in time to photograph these lovely flowers growing in the wild. They are native to these counties and many grow along the River Loddon, which also gives them its other name: Loddon Lily. Botanists have been puzzled as to why colonies were not discovered until the late eighteenth century, and there is now a controversy as to whether they are really native or not. It seems immaterial, and we are lucky still to have this beautiful bulb growing wild.

It will do well in the garden in any damp, shady area and soon develops into large clumps. I imagine it is called Summer Snowflake (despite the fact that it flowers in spring) because of its cousin, the Spring Snowflake (*L. vernum*) which flowers as early as February.

Lonicera periclymenum Honeysuckle ▲

P 6 m *June–October*

You must find room for at least one specimen of this robust climber. Let it grow only up a well-established tree, because otherwise it will strangle it, but better still find a wall, trellis or arbour up which it can grow. Also, make sure you get a true native specimen if buying a plant. A cutting or some seed from a hedgerow should be easy to establish. If possible, keep the roots in shade.

I still read how attractive Honeysuckle is to bees, but, when I observe them, the bees often seem to find the flowers awkward to get into. Moths, however, have no such problems; the strong night scent seems to attract them from a long way off and it is the major source of nectar for them. If you also have the larvae food plants available, you could end up with a wonderful variety of moths. You might also end up with some White Admiral butterflies as Honeysuckle is the larvae's most important food source.

Lotus corniculatus Common Bird's-foot-trefoil ▼

P 30 cm *June–September*

Very little needs to be said about this plant, which is widespread and will grow almost anywhere you care to put it. It is a plant much loved by all insects, as is its sprawling cousin, Greater Bird's-foot-trefoil.

The butterfly in the picture below is an Essex Skipper.

Lychnis flos-cuculi Ragged-robin ▼

P 90 cm *May–August*

Sadly, this flower seems to be declining, and I do not think anyone is quite sure exactly why, apart from the fact that much of its habitat of damp meadows has been lost. I used to have many colonies in the damp areas on the edge of my woodlands, but in recent years they have become less and less frequent. Ragged-robin is very suitable for planting along pond verges (see page 36–37). Cutting off the dead flowers will encourage a longer flowering season. It has untidy-looking flowers with petals waving all over the place, which nevertheless give it charm. Maybe it is that which also attracts very large numbers of butterflies and moths, including the Small Pearl-bordered Fritillary.

Malva moschata Musk-mallow ▼

P 60 cm *July–August*

Although this plant is perennial, it never seems to come up in the same place twice in my garden! I have found it in partial shade in the woods, struggling through brambles and nettles, on the edge of the lawn, and in rough ground just anywhere. It is one of the tallest and most conspicuous of our wild plants, and has been a cottage-garden favourite for a very long time. This is probably why it has a large number of cultivars, although the 'alba' version does occur in the wild.

I am sure you will have no difficulty in growing this mallow – it self-seeds quite freely. It prefers a sunny, well-drained site. I understand that the flowers, seeds and leaves can be used raw in salads, but I have never tried them.

Matthiola incana Hoary Stock ▲

P 90 cm *May–August*

This is the parent of the many stocks that you can now buy in garden centres. It is now also rare, in that it is confined to the chalk cliffs in my part of the world, namely Sussex, and also grows on the Isle of Wight. It is scented and will make a stunning show if massed in a border.

Rather oddly, the Red Data List of 2005 does not mention the plant at all, even under category LC (least concern). This must be an error, since quite widespread plants are listed. It does, however, list its cousin, *M. sinuata*, as 'vulnerable'.

Meconopsis cambrica Welsh Poppy ▶

P 60 cm *June–August*

There is some doubt as to whether the Welsh Poppy really belongs to the *Meconopsis* genus. It is the only one growing in Europe and very local at that: Wales and the west of Britain. The others all come from the Himalayas and mountains of China, and most are that glorious blue that few other flowers can emulate.

This was one of the species that I sowed in spring without success, but I think it may emerge the following year. Sow seeds or plant in light soil, preferably among rocks, thus emulating its natural habitat.

Melampyrum pratense Common Cow-wheat ▼

A 60 cm *May–October*

None of the cow-wheats are very widespread these days, not even the common one. Common Cow-wheat is an annual and an ancient-woodland indicator. Large swathes of it appear in a part of my woodland every year, and the fact that it is a woodland plant may have given it a much better chance of survival. The rare Heath Fritillary larvae feeds on this plant.

Field Cow-wheat, on the other hand, is another of those rare arable weeds that have been brought to near extinction by modern chemical farming methods (others include Cornflower, Corn Chamomile, Corncockle). Despite its rarity, Field Cow-wheat is only 'waiting' on the Red Data List. Waiting for what? For it to become extinct or to be classified as a neophyte?

Field Cow-wheat is an extravagant, handsome plant as well as being very rare, so it would be well worthwhile trying to grow it and if possible include it in a cornfield meadow.

Melampyrum arvense Field Cow-wheat ▼

A 60 cm *June–September*

Melittis melissophyllum Bastard Balm ▼

P 60 cm *May–July*

If you have a small woodland area, this is ideal for planting along the verges, where it will get some shade. Bastard Balm, also known as Honey Balm, belongs to the ubiquitous *Labiate* family, most of which have endearing faces and little platforms inviting insects to alight. Most of them are very small and need looking at closely to appreciate them fully. Not so Bastard Balm, whose flowers are large and handsome. It appreciates rich soil, is heavily scented, is loved by insects and is also rare.

Melica uniflora Wood Melick ▲

P 60 cm *May–July*

This is another ancient-woodland indicator and one of the most charming of all grasses. It is neither tall nor at all invasive, and its pretty sprays of flowers and seeds just ask to be sown in a shady spot.

Ononis repens Common Restharrow ▼

P 60 cm *June–September*

This is a very pretty pink flower belonging to the pea family. It is still reasonably common on grasslands, despite the fact that it used to annoy farmers in the days of horse and plough, because its extensive root system could completely entangle itself, especially in a harrow – hence the name. But its root system also contains many tiny white nodules that are full of nitrogen. Many legume plants are able to fix nitrogen from the air, and thus supply some of their own nutrients.

Restharrow is the preferred source of nectar for the Lulworth Skipper and food plant of the Common Blue.

Onobrychis viciifolia Sainfoin ▲

P 90 cm *June–September*

A wonderful plant for bees and bumblebees. It has a very long taproot and is therefore very drought-resistant. I had one in a large pot of clay soil and it produced wonderful spikes of bright, red-and-pink-veined flowers. It would be good for a grassland meadow, or on its own in a border.

Orchis mascula **Early-purple Orchid** ▲

0 60 cm *April–June*

Orchis simia **Monkey Orchid** ▲

0 60 cm *May–June*

With the exception of the Bee Orchid, all the orchids on these two pages belong to the Orchis group. There are four species of Ophrys in Britain of which the Bee Orchid is the most common. Like the other orchids on these pages, it is tuberous. The flowering tuber dies off every year but the plant may have grown one or more during the season, in which case you may have none or several the following year! It is therefore important to encourage self-seeding or collect and sow seeds yourself.

Orchids have fascinated botanists and others for centuries, not only because of the alluring flowers, but because of the devious ways many of them have evolved in order to attract insects to pollinate them. Darwin wrote a whole book on the subject, *The Various Contrivances by which Orchids are Fertilised by Insects. Ophrys* species often mimic the female of an insect in order to attract the male. In the case of the Bee Orchid, there are normally no honey bee males flying around (although there are much rarer mining bees, which are attracted by the pheromones the orchid exudes) so, if no other insect performs the task, it resorts to self-pollination, which it seems to do very successfully!

Orchis purpurea Lady Orchid ▼
0 90 cm *May–June*

Orchis ustulata Burnt Orchid ▲
0 30 cm *May–June*

Ophrys apifera Bee Orchid ▲
0 60 cm *June–July*

I am lucky to have a meadow of the Early-purple Orchid growing in my woods — I egged on a few of them by clearing brambles and they appear to have responded with gusto. The other four orchids are all very rare and restricted to only a few remaining sites. Even if you find some, do not collect seeds. They are also some of the most beautiful, and, sadly, they have become so rare due indiscriminate picking and digging up in the past. Nevertheless, I have included them because I feel sure that, by the time this book is published, some, if not all, will be available as plants. Even if you can locate any Monkey or Military Orchids, do not attempt to collect seeds: it requires a special permit.

Orobanche hederae Ivy Broomrape ▼

P 60 cm *June–July*

Broomrapes are singular plants. There are about 150 species in the world: all of them are parasitic and nine of them occur in Britain. None of them are common and they all have their individual host plants. Chlorophyll is absent from all of them, resulting in unusual-looking plants of all hues except green. One of the other British broomrapes is Yorkshire or Thistle Broomrape (*Orobanche reticulata*), which lives off the Creeping Thistle. You might well think it would be a useful plant, keeping this invasive one at bay. I am afraid not – none of the broomrapes seem to damage the host plant.

Ivy Broomrape, as its name implies, is dependent on our native ivy, *Hedera helix*, and is very scarce, although seeds can be purchased. Small insects will pollinate broomrapes.

Origanum vulgare Wild Marjoram ▲

P 90 cm *July–September*

It would be difficult to find a better plant for attracting wildlife. Butterflies, bees, bumblebees, hoverflies and many other insects seem to be especially drawn to the flowers of our native culinary herbs such as Chives, Parsley, Thyme and Wild Garlic, but the most popular is Wild Marjoram. Often, when these plants are grown for culinary use, the flowers tend to be cut so lush leaves can be harvested. But, if you want to attract the wildlife, you must let at least some of them flower – in any case, the flowers are just as good added to stews, soups and salads. My herb patch is a vast tangle of everything, and whenever I go there in midsummer it is literally buzzing, all of which ceases when I try to get close for a photograph!

Oxalis acetosella Wood-sorrel ◄

P 10 cm *April–June*

There are few plants that have had as much written about them as the charming Wood Sorrel – writers and poets have sung its praises, it seems to have a host of medicinal and culinary uses, and also great debates exist as to whether it is the true Irish Shamrock or one of several clovers or trefoils. It is certainly an enchanting woodland plant that goes to sleep at night, spreads through rhizomes and appears among moss, in the cleft of trees or along the woodland floor.

Petasites hybridus Butterbur ▼

P 90 cm *March–May*

Sometimes the leaves of this plant can attain a width of almost a metre, so it is not surprising that they are sometimes mistaken for rhubarb. The unmistakable flowers emerge very early in the year. Butterburs are common in wet places and along rivers and can sometimes be found in large colonies that have spread through the underground rhizomes.

Osmunda regalis Royal Fern ▲

P 3 m *June–August*

This is a tall, majestic fern that should do well anywhere with sufficient moisture, even on a sunny site. If you grow it by a pond, keep the crowns out of the water. It is a large plant, so allow plenty of room for it to expand. Mature plants will produce tall spikes of rusty-coloured spore-bearing flowers in late summer.

Primula farinosa Bird's-eye Primrose ▶

P 10 cm *May–August*

I have to confess that I have never seen this pink member of the primrose family in the wild – probably because it is frequent only in the Yorkshire Dales, where it grows on limestone grassland. However, I do not think it would be difficult to establish it elsewhere and one wonders what a collection of these and Yellow Primroses would look like.

Pulsatilla vulgaris Pasqueflower ▲

P 10 cm *April–June*

I do not think any garden of wild flowers should be without Pasqueflowers, surely one of our most beautiful plants and one that is becoming increasingly scarce in the wild. Even when it is not in flower, the graceful lace-like leaves look attractive on their own. Seeds and plants are readily available, but, again, do make sure you get the real native species. If you can obtain fresh, ripe seeds, sow them immediately because once they become dormant they may be tricky to germinate. Once they are established, do not move or break up clumps. Beware, slugs and snails also love Pasqueflowers!

Ranunculus tripartitus Three-lobed Crowfoot ▼

A/P floating *Mar–July*

This is a rare member of the Buttercup family and is listed as vulnerable in the Red Data list. It is only practical in the garden if you can give it an area of shallow water all to itself, since it resents competition from other plants. In fact a 'puddle' that remains filled with water all year would be ideal. There are many Water-Crowfoots, some with clover-like leaves like this one and others with feather-like leaves, but all have white flowers. Like all aquatic plants, it provides a habitat for larvae and nymphs.

Below it is another unusual member of the Buttercup family, the Celery-leaved Buttercup (*Ranunculus sceleratus*), which grows in wet places such as ditches and bogs. It is not as rare as the Crowfoot, but beware: it is very poisonous!

Reseda lutea Wild Mignonette ▲

P/Bi 90 cm *Jun–September*

This is one of the ten seeds I sowed once I learned I was going to write this book. It was reasonably successful and existing plants are providing seeds for future ones. Although it prefers chalky soils, it is doing quite well on my clay. It would look good as a group in a border, but I would eventually like to see mine in a meadow. Reference books do not seem to agree whether it is an annual, biennual or perennial – mine certainly flowered in the first year and look like continuing into the next. It is faintly scented and a great attractant for insects.

Rhinanthus minor Yellow-rattle ▶

<u>**A**</u> 60 cm *May–September*

Yellow-rattle is definitely a plant you should grow if you are contemplating any kind of meadow or border that is likely to contain unwanted or coarse grasses. It is called a hemi-parasite, in that it feeds off the roots of various grasses and can therefore exert some control over them. Do not think, however, that you can grow it on your lawn and that it will get rid of all the grasses!

It is a strange-looking plant with large 'purses' from which relatively small flowers emerge. When these disappear, the stem is left with many brown bladders, which contain the seeds that rattle in the wind. It will grow almost anywhere but prefers full sun.

Ribes spicatum Downy Currant ▼

<u>**P**</u> 1.5 m *April–May*

This is a rare little shrub, which grows in my woodland and rather surprisingly in a very overgrown boggy area. I rarely manage to see it with fruit, yet alone photograph it, because invariably birds have got there before me! Like all plants that bear fruit, it is wonderful for wildlife, and would it not make a change growing a fruit you do not have to protect from birds?

Reseda luteola Weld ▲

<u>**Bi**</u> 1.5 m *June–September*

Weld is closely related to Wild Mignonette and can look very attractive in gardens. It is biennial and can grow up to 1.5 m. It also attracts many insects, among them the Bath White and Small White butterflies. Beware of the latter, because it is one of the two that will decimate brassicas in the vegetable plot. It is also an important plant for dyers, producing rich yellow and orange dyes; mixed with Woad (*Isatis tinctoria*), which is not a native plant, it produces a green dye.

Rosa arvensis **Field-rose** ◄▲
P 3 m *June–August*
Rosa pimpinellifolia **Burnet Rose** ▼
P 1 m *May–July*

Rosa canina Dog-rose ▶

P 5 m *June–August*

Rosa rubiginosa Sweet-briar ▼

P 3 m *June–July*

Some wild roses can be lethal with long arching stems covered in strong thorns, so handle with care, even with gloves. There are quite a number of native species, of which the Field and Dog Rose are the most abundant. Burnet Rose is much smaller and grows best on chalky soil and has large, round, black hips. Sweet Briar is erect-growing, more uncommon and also known as Eglantine of Shakespearean fame. Puck's speech from *A Midsummer Night's Dream* evokes a marvellous picture of wild plants:

> *I know a bank whereon the wild thyme blows,*
> *Where oxlips and the nodding violet grows*
> *Quite over-canopied with luscious woodbine,*
> *With sweet musk-roses, and with eglantine …*

Needless to say, wild roses are used by an astonishing number of wildlife, both the nectar and hips providing food, especially the latter in midwinter, when other food is scarce.

Rubus fruticosus agg. **Bramble Raspberry** ▼

P 3 m *May–September*

The abbreviation 'agg.' after the Latin name stands for aggregate, which really means that even botanists sometimes do not know which bramble they are looking at. There are more than 300 species in Britain known as microspecies, and they have so many ways of successfully propagating themselves that I think nothing needs to be said about how to grow them.

Brambles are widespread, certainly in the southern half of Britain, and are positively rampant in my woods and garden, so much so that they infuriate me when they oust much smaller, more delicate plants. However, one has to temper this with the fact that they are one of the best plants for wildlife, especially in bloom and when they fruit (many never bear fruit inside a mature woodland). If you can, do grow at least one up a sunny wall or fence. Birds love the fruit, as do all kinds of mammals – even my dogs delicately pick them off. The nectar in the flowers attracts almost any insect, even, as you can see, butterflies – a Green Veined White in this case.

Rumex acetosa **Common Sorrel** ▲

P 90 cm *May–June*

Docks and sorrels are important to many insects, especially the Small Copper butterfly, whose larvae feed on the leaves. You may not think them very attractive for the garden, but in fact groups of Sorrel in flower can be quite eye-catching. The problem is that they can spread very rapidly, but, if you watch out for the small seedlings, they are easily removed. They also have others uses: they are really quite effective against nettle stings.

Scabiosa columbaria Small Scabious ▶

P 60 cm *July–August*

There are three species of scabious: Devil's-bit (*Succisa pratensis*), Field (*Knautia arvensis*) and this one. They all belong to the Teasel family and all have similar blue flowers. You should have no problems establishing them from either seed or plants, and you should endeavour to have a good group, because they are very important to wildlife. The nectar is preferred by a host of insects, including butterflies – normally they all fly off when I try to photograph a plant close up. The particular hoverfly in the picture was obviously drunk with nectar – nothing would budge it!

Scilla verna Spring Squill ▶

P 30 cm *April–June*

The close relative of Spring Squill is the Autumn variety (*Scilla autumnalis*). Both prefer coastlines: the spring variety grows as far north as the Shetlands, whereas the Autumn Squill grows best in the wild only in Devon and Cornwall. Bulbs are wonderfully useful in gardens, requiring little maintenance. Ones that come up in spring and autumn, especially these pretty ones, are an added bonus.

Scirpus sylvaticus Wood Club-rush ◀

P 1.2 m *May–July*

There are a huge number or rushes and sedges inhabiting various wetlands, and many are becoming increasingly popular for garden cultivation. Wood Club-rush is an ancient-woodland indicator, and I have large swathes of them in the wet part of my woods. I find them very attractive both in flower and in seed, but you should be careful not to let them become invasive. They spread rapidly – as soon as a tree comes down in the bog, they rush in to populate the light space.

Sedum telephium Orpine ▶

P 90 cm *July–September*

Many gardeners who want to attract wildlife will already have one or more of the Stonecrop family, but the chances are that it will be something like *Sedum spectabile*, the butterfly plant, not a native. This wild species is not overly common and, like the garden varieties, will attract insects and butterflies. The fleshy leaves denote that it is very drought-resistant. Unfortunately, my picture only shows the plant in bud (I paid it frequent visits, but it was never in full bloom!), which eventually opens bright pink.

Senecio jacobaea Common Ragwort ▼

P/Bi 90 cm *June–November*

I feel Ragwort is somewhat unjustly persecuted. When dried, and I stress when dried as hay, it can make cattle and horses very ill. But it has to be a very stupid animal that will eat it while it is growing. I have a couple of old sheep and two Shetland ponies who frequently graze where Ragwort is growing, but I have never known them to touch it. In flower, Ragwort is extremely conspicuous, although that is not the reason why the flamboyant Cinnabar moth has chosen it as its favourite plant on which to lay eggs. It is because the resultant larvae are well camouflaged against predators from above, as can be seen in the picture.

Seseli libanotis Moon Carrot ▼

P/Bi 90 cm *July–September*

This is a rare but robust species of the ubiquitous umbellifers. One of its strongholds is along the chalky grasslands of southern England. I searched in vain for it along Beachy Head, but without success. It is a good garden plant (seeds and plugs are available), whose flower stems, growing as a rosette, often reach a height of one metre.

Silene spp. Campions

This is a sizable group of plants, mostly bright-pink- and white-flowering, which includes all the catchflies.

Red Campion is widespread but also very popular. It will grow along shady borders and even under trees, spreading rapidly via underground rhizomes, and will not fail to make a good show. It looks lovely among bluebells, cuckoo and other spring flowers. White Campion is less common but will hybridize with the red.

Bladder Campion is largely known for the way children will pop the calyx even before the flower opens. Both the White and Bladder Campions are extraordinarily popular among moths, but more familiar will be the froghoppers – those creatures that produce the white spittle on plants.

Silene dioica Red Campion ▷
P/Bi 90 cm *May–November*

Silene latifolia White Campion ◁
A/P 90 cm *May–October*

Silene vulgaris Bladder Campion ▽
P 90 cm *June–August*

Stachys palustris Marsh Woundwort ▲
P 90 cm *June–October*

Spiranthes spiralis Autumn Lady's-tresses ▲

O 30 cm *August–September*

I am not sure that I should really include this diminutive orchid, since it can apparently take eleven or more years to flower from seed! However, I understand some are being grown under laboratory conditions and I feel sure plug plants will be available soon. It is a rare orchid under threat of extinction, but you may find plants growing on chalky, dry grassland, especially in the southern half of England.

Stachys sylvatica Hedge Woundwort ▶

P 1.2 m *June–September*

I am fascinated by the woundworts. Both these and others in the same group seem very insignificant when you first come across them. However, a closer look, especially with a magnifying glass, reveals these wonderfully structured flowers that would do justice to any orchid, if only they were larger. As the name implies, they were used for a host of medicinal cures, but tiny insects also find them much to their liking. You should have no difficulty in growing them and I hope you will find a place for them and their cousin Betony (*stachys officinalis*) in the garden.

Symphytum officinale Common Comfrey ▶

P 1.2 m *May–July*

Comfrey must be one of the most versatile plants you can
grow in the garden. Not only is it extremely easy to grow,
but is an attractant for all kinds of wildlife, can be used for
dozens of cures in herbal medicine, and can be fed to
grazing animals. If composted it is rich in all kinds of
nutrients.

Tamus communis Black Bryony ▲

P 4 m *May–August*

This medley of red berries come from two plants: the small
ones from Cotoneaster (*Cotoneaster horizontalis*), which is
not native, and the large ones from Black Bryony. Every red
berry that I can think of is food for birds, and two of our
migrant winter visitors, Fieldfare and the incredible little
songster the Blackcap, are also partial to these berries. Birds
are extremely clever, not least where food is concerned. They
know exactly which berries and food will persist into late
winter and will save them up for these lean times. They also
know what is and is not poisonous.

The whole of Black Bryony is mildly poisonous to
humans (although parts have been eaten in the past) but not
to birds. For example, Yew berries are highly poisonous, but
only the seed: birds know this, eat the flesh and spit out the
seed, which, incidentally, enables the tree to propagate more
widely. I do not know whether they eat the whole of the
Black Bryony berries.

Black Bryony has male and female on separate plants, so,
if you want berries, make sure you have both.

Taraxacum officinale Dandelion ▶

P 40 cm *March–October*

Dandelions are extremely common and persistent plants
that have a long flowering season but are also very
underrated. They attract an enormous amount of wildlife in

the form of food for caterpillars, butterflies, moths, bees and
many others, and, like Colt's Foot, they can be eaten and are
much used in herbal medicine. In cultivation, they can
become very showy plants, and clever, too: they will grow
upright leaves if competing with tall plants, or flatten
themselves into rosettes if cut on lawns.

Trientalis europaea Chickweed-wintergreen ▼

P 30 cm *June–July*

This pretty little flower rarely grows in England but is common on moors and conifer woods in Scotland. It multiplies by creeping rhizomes. An interesting experiment was carried out with Chickweed Wintergreen: it is very susceptible to a smut fungus, *Urocystis trientalis*, and it was discovered that voles, who are partial to this plant, were even more partial to the infected leaves, thus reducing the spread of the fungus. This is not exactly biological control, but there is surely a moral in the tale.

Umbilicus rupestris Navelwort ▲

P 60 cm *June–August*

This member of the Stonecrop family is also known as Wall Pennywort – maybe a more descriptive name. When I was hunting for wild plants in Cornwall, I found these enchanting plants growing out of rocks and up walls everywhere. When life was less sophisticated, children used to play with the leaves, pretending they were coins. I am told the penny-sized leaves (before the flowering stems appear) are very good to eat. A pretty, mottled, straw-coloured moth, the Weaver's Wave, rests by day on damp walls and rocks, and uses the plant for its larvae.

Urtica dioica Common Nettle ▼

P 90 cm *June September*

Nature would sorely miss this plant despite the fact that it
stings (all humans and mammals) and can make a thorough
nuisance of itself. But it is very high in nitrogen and not
only can you eat it (salads and soups) and use it as a
medicine, but organic vegetable gardeners make manure
from it and heat up compost heaps. It also brings huge
advantages to the world of insects. For many butterflies and
moths it is the preferred plant on which to lay their eggs –
butterflies that include Painted Lady, Comma and Peacock,
and moths that include Burnished Brass and Beautiful
Golden Y, to name but a few. Other insects find it a good
source of shelter; browsing deer and cattle will eat virtually
everything, but growing nettles (and therefore the insects)
are left unmolested. Mammals will, however, relish nettles
once they are cut. Quite what the two Ruddy Darter
dragonflies found attractive in nettles is another matter!

Veronica anagallis-aquatica Blue-water Speedwell ▲

P 60 cm *June–August*

There are many Veronica species and everyone knows the
common or garden Germander Speedwell (*V. chamaedrys*),
whose flowers have incredibly sweet faces. Maybe these two,
which inhabit riverbanks and marshes, are not quite as
familiar. Blue Water grows upright, but Brooklime (its
brilliant blue is unmistakable) grows flat on water with
fleshy leaves under which tiny aquatic creatures can hide.
They are good plants for in and around a pond.

Veronica beccabunga Brooklime ◄

P 60 cm *May–September*

Viola spp **Violets**

There are hundreds of violet and pansy species, about a dozen of which are native, and all are important to wildlife. The Wild Pansy, also known as Heartsease, despite the fact that medicinally it is mainly used for skin conditions – and the Americans for some reason call it Johnny-Jump-Up – forms delightful clumps in sun or shade.

The Hairy Violet (so called because its leaves are hairy) is a chalk grassland plant and the Marsh Violet prefers bogs – two habitats that have been declining and with them these two species. It also partly explains the decline of many of the Fritillary butterflies, some of which rely on them, as well as the Early Dog-violet, for the main source of food for their larvae. They include the very rare (at least in the southern half of England) Small Pearl-bordered Fritillary, and also the Dark Green and Silver-washed Fritillary.

Given the right conditions, all these four violets are not difficult to grow: the Marsh Violet is a shy little plant and seems to hide away in wet shade, while the other three will tolerate quite a lot of sun. None of them are happy in dry conditions and all of them will spread quite rapidly via underground rhizomes.

Verbascum nigrum **Dark Mullein** ▲

P 90 cm *July–October*

The larvae of the now rare Striped Lychnis moth feed on Dark Mullein. The moth is currently confined to a few counties in the southern half of England, and the plant also is only relatively frequent on limestone in the south and east. It would be wonderful to think you could contribute to bringing back this moth by growing Dark Mullein in quantity, but I fear this may be wishful thinking. Incidentally, the moth larvae are a beautiful grey with black and yellow stripes. However, Dark Mullein is a plant well worth growing just for itself, quite apart from the fact it also is steeped in legends and folklore as well as a herbal medicine. Mullein in your shoes should prevent colds and some in your pocket will attract love!

Viola hirta Hairy Violet ▼
P 10 cm *March–June*

Viola tricolor Wild Pansy ◄
A/P 30 cm *April–October*
Viola palustris Marsh Violet ▲
P 10 cm *April–July*

Viola reichenbachiana Early Dog-violet ▲
P 10 cm *March–June*

4

Complete List

THE COMPLETE LIST OF NATIVE SPECIES OF
the Botanical Society of the British Isles (BSBI)

The following is a comprehensive list of native
plants, complete with details of type, height,
flowering times and habitats. The final column
gives page numbers where the plants are
mentioned elsewhere in the book.

KEY

T *tree*   **P** *perennial* (including shrubs)
A *annual*   **Bi** *biennial* **O** *orchid*
No subspecies or hybrids are included.

BOTANICAL NAME	COMMON NAME	TYPE	MAX. HEIGHT	FLOWERS	HABITATS	PAGE
Acer campestre	Field Maple	T	up to 20 m	Apr–May	Hedgerows, open woods and coppices	
Aceras anthropophorum	Man Orchid	O	up to 30 cm	May–Jun	Chalky, grassy banks, open scrub, field edges	
Achillea millefolium	Yarrow	P	up to 60 cm	Jul–Oct	Chalky, slightly acid, meadows, road verges, waste	
Achillea ptarmica	Sneezewort	P	up to 90 cm	Jul–Sep	Acid, neutral soils, marshes, meadows, stream banks	42
Aconitum napellus	Monk's-hood	P	up to 90 cm	Jun–Sep	Damp, meadows, woodland, stream banks	42
Actaea spicata	Baneberry	P	up to 60 cm	May–Jul	Woods over limestone rocks in fissures	
Adiantum capillus-veneris	Maidenhair Fern	P	up to 15 cm	May–Sep	Rare, western limestone sea cliffs	
Adoxa moschatellina	Moschatel	P	up to 10 cm	Apr–May	Damp soils, shady places	
Aethusa cynapium	Fool's Parsley	Bi	up to 60 cm	Jun–Oct	Arable land, waste places, open woods	
Agrimonia eupatoria	Agrimony	P	up to 60 cm	Jun–Aug	Slightly acid to chalky, dry grassy places, field edges	
Agrimonia procera	Fragrant Agrimony	P	up to 90 cm	Jun–Aug	Grassy, scrub, heavy moist soils	
Agrostis canina	Velvet Bent	P	up to 70 cm	Jun–Jul	Damp, meadows, heaths, pond edges	
Agrostis capillaris	Common Bent	P	up to 70 cm	Jun–Aug	Fields, heaths	
Agrostis curtisii	Bristle Bent	P	up to 60 cm	Jun–Jul	Heaths, moors	
Agrostis gigantea	Black Bent	P	up to 1.5 m	Jun–Aug	Arable, grassy banks, open woods	
Agrostis stolonifera	Creeping Bent	P	up to 2 m	Jul–Aug	Waste places, grassland	
Agrostis vinealis	Brown Bent	P	up to 70 cm	Jun–Aug	Heaths, moors	
Aira caryophyllea	Silver Hair-grass	A	up to 50 cm	May–Jul	Sandy soils, dry places, walls	
Aira praecox	Early Hair-grass	A	up to 10 cm	Mar–Jun	Sandy soils, dry places, walls, sand dunes	
Ajuga chamaepitys	Ground-pine	A	up to 30 cm	May–Sep	Chalky, stony ground, sparse grassy habitats	
Ajuga pyramidalis	Pyramidal Bugle	P	up to 30 cm	Apr–Aug	Chalky, rocky ground, sparse grassy habitats	
Ajuga reptans	Bugle	P	up to 30 cm	Apr–Jun	Chalky to slightly acid, waste, woodland	
Alchemilla alpina	Alpine Lady's-mantle	P	up to 30 cm	Jun–Aug	Mountains, acid soil	
Alchemilla filicaulis	Hairy Lady's-mantle	P	up to 30 cm	Jun–Sep	Common, mountains	
Alchemilla glabra	Smooth Lady's-mantle	P	up to 60 cm	Jun–Sep	Open woodland, grassy and rocky areas	
Alchemilla xanthochlora	Intermediate Lady's-mantle	P	up to 60 cm	May–Jul	Mainly grassy areas at low altitude	
Alisma gramineum	Ribbon-leaved Water-plantain	P	up to 90 cm	Jul–Sep	Rare, known area: Worcs	
Alisma lanceolatum	Narrow-leaved Water-plantain	P	up to 90 cm	Jun–Aug	Widespread except far north	
Alisma plantago-aquatica	Water-plantain	P	up to 90 cm	Jun–Aug	Widespread except far north	
Alliaria petiolata	Garlic Mustard	Bi	up to 90 cm	Apr–Jun	Chalky, rich soils, common roadsides, waste ground	
Allium ampeloprasum	Wild Leek	P	up to 1.8 m	Jul–Aug	Sea, hedgerows, rocky	
Allium oleraceum	Field Garlic	P	up to 90 cm	Jun–Aug	Roadside, scrub, rocky, cult. land	
Allium schoenoprasum	Chives	P	up to 60 cm	Jun–Aug	Grass, rocky habitats, stream beds	
Allium scorodoprasum	Sand Leek	P	up to 90 cm	Jun–Aug	Sandy, hedgerows, waste ground, cultivated land	
Allium sphaerocephalon	Round-headed Leek	P	up to 90 cm	Jun–Aug	Rocky, grassy areas	
Allium ursinum	Ramsons	P	up to 60 cm	Apr–Jun	Hedgerows, scrub, woodland	43
Allium vineale	Wild Onion	P	up to 1.2 m	Jun–Aug	Dry, rocky, grassy, road verges, waste	
Alnus glutinosa	Alder	T	up to 20 m	Feb–Apr	Widespread often by freshwater	
Alopecurus aequalis	Orange Foxtail	A	up to 40 cm	Jun–Sep	Pond, marginal	
Alopecurus borealis	Alpine Foxtail	P	up to 30 cm	Jun–Aug	Mountains, wet areas	
Alopecurus bulbosus	Bulbous Foxtail	P	up to 40 cm	May–Aug	Salt marshes	
Alopecurus geniculatus	Marsh Foxtail	P	up to 45 cm	Jun–Jul	Wet areas, lakes, rivers	
Alopecurus myosuroides	Black-grass	A	up to 85 cm	May–Aug	Arable, waste land	
Alopecurus pratensis	Meadow Foxtail	P	up to 1.1 m	Apr–Jun	Damp meadows, grassland	
Althaea officinalis	Marsh-mallow	P	up to 2 m	Aug–Sep	Coastal, marshes, ditches, streams	44
Ammophila arenaria	Marram	P	up to 1.2 cm	Jul–Aug	Common, sand dunes	
Anacamptis pyramidalis	Pyramidal Orchid	O	up to 60 cm	Jun–Aug	Meadows, pastures, roadsides, banks	22, 23, 44
Anagallis arvensis	Scarlet Pimpernel	A	up to 10 cm	May–Oct	Sandy, light soils, waste ground, coastal dunes	45
Anagallis minima	Chaffweed	A	up to 10 cm	Jun–Aug	Sandy heaths, commons, coastal dunes	
Anagallis tenella	Bog Pimpernel	P	up to 10 cm	May–Sep	Damp areas, bogs, marshes	
Anchusa arvensis	Bugloss	A	up to 60 cm	Apr–Sep	Sandy heaths, waste and arable land	
Andromeda polifolia	Bog-rosemary	P	up to 35 cm	May–Sep	Wet acid habitats, bogs	45
Anemone nemorosa	Wood Anemone	P	up to 30 cm	Mar–May	Woodland, clearings, scrub, hedgerows	45
Angelica sylvestris	Wild Angelica	P	up to 90 cm	Jul–Aug	Wet habitats, fens, meadows, woods	46
Anisantha sterilis	Barren Brome	A/Bi	up to 90 cm	May–Jul	Hedgerows, roadsides, waste and cultivated ground	
Anogramma leptophylla	Jersey Fern	A	up to 20 cm	Mar–May	Rare, Jersey, Guernsey	
Antennaria dioica	Mountain Everlasting	P	up to 30 cm	May–Jul	Chalky, rich soils, mountain grassland	
Anthemis arvensis	Corn Chamomile	A	up to 60 cm	Jun–Jul	Road verges, waste, arable and cultivated ground	30
Anthemis cotula	Stinking Chamomile	A	up to 60 cm	May–Oct	Waste, arable, stubble, farmyards	
Anthoxanthum odoratum	Sweet Vernal-grass	P	up to 50 cm	Apr–Jul	Grassland, pastures, heaths	
Anthriscus caucalis	Bur Chervil	A	up to 90 cm	May–Jun	Dry, sandy soils, waste, hedge banks	
Anthriscus sylvestris	Cow Parsley	Bi/P	up to 1.5 m	Apr–Jun	Grassy, hedgerows, waste	
Anthyllis vulneraria	Kidney Vetch	P	up to 60 cm	Jun–Sep	Dry coastal cliffs, rocks, grasslands	46
Apera interrupta	Dense Silky-bent	A	up to 70 cm	Jun–Jul	Sandy soil, waste, cult. land	
Apera spica-venti	Loose Silky-bent	A	up to 100 cm	Jun–Aug	Waste, sandy fields	
Aphanes arvensis	Parsley-piert	A	up to 30 cm	Apr–Oct	Waste and arable, roadsides	
Aphanes inexspectata	Slender Parsley-piert	A	up to 30 cm	Apr–Oct	Commons, heaths, grass, woodland	
Apium graveolens	Wild Celery	Bi	up to 90 cm	Jun–Aug	Wet, riverbanks, ditches, salt meadows	

BOTANICAL NAME	COMMON NAME	TYPE	MAX. HEIGHT	FLOWERS	HABITATS	PAGE
Apium inundatum	Lesser Marshwort	P	up to 60 cm	Jun–Aug	Wet, still and slow water	
Apium nodiflorum	Fool's-water-cress	P	up to 60 cm	Jul–Aug	Wet, chalky soils, widespread	
Apium repens	Creeping Marshwort	P	up to 60 cm	Jul–Aug	Wet, pools, ditches, meadows	
Aquilegia vulgaris	Columbine	P	up to 90 cm	May–Jul	Grassy banks, scrub, woodland	46
Arabidopsis thaliana	Thale Cress	A/Bi	up to 60 cm	Mar–Oct	Hedgerows, banks, walls waste and cultivated land	
Arabis alpina	Alpine Rock-cress	P	up to 30 cm	May–Jul	Wet mountain, rocks ledges screes	
Arabis glabra	Tower Mustard	Bi	up to 90 cm	May–Jul	Dry, heaths, open woods	
Arabis hirsuta	Hairy Rock-cress	Bi	up to 60 cm	May–Aug	Dry, rocks, walls, dunes, grassland	
Arabis petraea	Northern Rock-cress	P	up to 30 cm	Jun–Aug	Mountains, river gravels, screes	
Arabis scabra	Bristol Rock-cress	P	up to 30 cm	Mar–May	Cliffs, rocks, screes	
Arbutus unedo	Strawberry-tree	T	up to 8 m	Aug–Dec	Scrub, rocky, woodland margins	
Arctium lappa	Greater Burdock	Bi	up to 1.5 m	Jul–Sep	Hedgerows, waste, open woodland	
Arctium minus	Lesser Burdock	Bi	up to 1.5 m	Jul–Sep	All habitats, except acid soils	
Arctostaphylos alpinus	Alpine Bearberry	P	up to 60 cm	May–Aug	Mountain, heaths, moors	
Arctostaphylos uva-ursi	Bearberry	P	up to 1.5 m	Jul–Sep	Peaty soils, open woodland, heaths, moors	
Arenaria ciliata	Fringed Sandwort	P	up to 10 cm	Jul–Aug	Rocky habitats, meadows	
Arenaria norvegica	Arctic Sandwort	P	up to 10 cm	May–Jul	Screes, river gravels, stony	
Arenaria serpyllifolia	Thyme-leaved Sandwort	A	up to 30 cm	Apr–Sep	Sandy dry, walls, heaths	
Armeria arenaria	Jersey Thrift	P	up to 60 cm	May–Sep	Sea cliffs, dry grassland	
Armeria maritima	Thrift	P	up to 30 cm	Apr–Aug	Sea cliffs, meadows, marshes	47
Arnoseris minima	Lamb's Succory	A	up to 30 cm	Jun–Aug	Sandy waste and cultivated soils	
Arrhenatherum elatius	False Oat-grass	P	up to 1.5 m	Jun–Sep	Grassy banks, roadsides	
Artemisia absinthium	Wormwood	P	up to 90 cm	Jul–Aug	Sandy, coastal, road verges, waste ground	
Artemisia campestris	Field Wormwood	P	up to 90 cm	Aug–Sep	Sandy, roadsides, waste, arable	
Artemisia norvegica	Norwegian Mugwort	P	up to 30 cm	Jul–Sep	Mountain, rocks	
Artemisia vulgaris	Mugwort	P	up to 90 cm	May–Sep	Hedgerows, roadsides, riverbanks	
Arum italicum	Italian Lords-and-Ladies	P	up to 60 cm	May–Jun	Hedgerows, roadsides	47
Arum maculatum	Lords-and-Ladies	P	up to 30 cm	Apr–May	Hedgerows, banks, woodland	47
Asparagus officinalis	Wild Asparagus	P	up to 1.2 m	Jun–Aug	Scrub, grassy, waste, cultivated land	
Asperula cynanchica	Squinancywort	P	up to 25 cm	Jun–Sep	Dry pastures, grass dunes	
Asplenium adiantum-nigrum	Black Spleenwort	P	up to 50 cm	Jun–Oct	Rocky, banks, walls, crevices	
Asplenium marinum	Sea Spleenwort	P	up to 30 cm	Jun–Oct	Sea, rock crevices	
Asplenium obovatum	Lanceolate Spleenwort	P	up to 30 cm	Jul–Oct	Rocks, walls, hedge banks	
Asplenium onopteris	Irish Spleenwort	P	up to 50 cm	Jul–Oct	Limestone, rocks, walls	
Asplenium ruta-muraria	Wall-rue	P	up to 10 cm	Jun–Oct	Rocks, limestone walls, bridges	
Asplenium septentrionale	Forked Spleenwort	P	up to 15 cm	Jun–Oct	Rare, rock crevices	
Asplenium trichomanes	Maidenhair Spleenwort	P	up to 20 cm	May–Oct	Common, rocks, walls	48
Asplenium trichomanes-ramosum	Green Spleenwort	P	up to 15 cm	Jun–Sep	Common, limestone rocks mountains	
Aster linosyris	Goldilocks Aster	P	up to 60 cm	Aug–Sep	Grassland cliffs	
Aster tripolium	Sea Aster	A	up to 60 cm	Jul–Aug	Coastal, saline	
Astragalus alpinus	Alpine Milk-vetch	P	up to 30 cm	Jul–Aug	Rocky cliffs, mountain grass	
Astragalus danicus	Purple Milk-vetch	P	up to 30 cm	May–Jul	Limestone, coastal dunes, grass meadows	48
Astragalus glycyphyllos	Wild Liquorice	P	up to 90 cm	Jun–Aug	Scrub, roadside, rough grass, open woods	48
Athyrium distentifolium	Alpine Lady-fern	P	up to 1.5 m	Jul–Aug	Uncommon, mountain, rocks, screes	
Athyrium filix-femina	Lady-fern	P	up to 1.5 m	Jul–Aug	Common, damp, marshes, woods, hedgerows	49
Athyrium flexile	Newman's Lady-fern	P	up to 30 cm	May–Jul	Mountains	
Atriplex glabriuscula	Babington's Orache	A	up to 30 cm	Jul–Aug	Sea, sandy, shingle shores	
Atriplex laciniata	Frosted Orache	A	up to 30 cm	Jul–Sep	Coastal, sand dunes, shingle	
Atriplex littoralis	Grass-leaved Orache	A	up to 90 cm	Jul–Oct	Sea, salt marshes	
Atriplex longipes	Long-stalked Orache	A	up to 80 cm	Jul–Oct	Salt marshes	
Atriplex patula	Common Orache	A	up to 90 cm	Jul–Oct	Seashores, waste, cultivated land	
Atriplex pedunculata	Pedunculate Sea-purslane	A	up to 60 cm	Jun–Sep	Coastal, salt marshes	
Atriplex portulacoides	Sea-purslane	P	up to 60 cm	Jul–Oct	Sea, salt marshes	
Atriplex praecox	Early Orache	A	up to 10 cm	Jul–Oct	Coastal, shingle, meadows	
Atriplex prostrata	Spear-leaved Orache	A	up to 90 cm	Jul–Oct	Coastal, sand, shingle, roadsides	
Atropa belladonna	Deadly Nightshade	P	up to 1.5 m	Jun–Aug	Damp, shady woods, scrub, rocky	49
Baldellia ranunculoides	Lesser Water-plantain	P	up to 30 cm	Jun–Sep	Aquatic, freshwater, streams, ponds	
Ballota nigra	Black Horehound	P	up to 90 cm	Jun–Sep	Roadsides, hedge banks, waste ground	
Barbarea stricta	Small-flowered Winter-cress	Bi	up to 90 cm	May–Aug	Damp, riverbanks, road verges, waste ground	
Barbarea vulgaris	Winter-cress	Bi/P	up to 90 cm	May–Aug	Damp, ditches, riverbanks, hedgerows	
Bartsia alpina	Alpine Bartsia	P	up to 30 cm	Jun–Aug	Wet, mountain pastures	
Bellis perennis	Daisy	P	up to 10 cm	Mar–Oct	Common, grassy places	
Berberis vulgaris	Barberry	P	up to 3 m	May–Jun	Dry, chalky, woods, scrub, rocky, hedgerows	
Berula erecta	Lesser Water-parsnip	P	up to 90 cm	Jul–Sep	Semi-aquatic, freshwater	
Beta vulgaris	Beet	Bi	up to 90 cm	Jun–Sep	Seashores, shingle, sea walls	
Betula nana	Dwarf Birch	T	up to 1 m	Jun–Jul	Woods, bogs, moors	
Betula pendula	Silver Birch	T	up to 30 m	Apr–May	Woods, heaths	
Betula pubescens	Downy Birch	T	up to 20 m	Apr–May	Damp heaths	

BOTANICAL NAME	COMMON NAME	TYPE	MAX. HEIGHT	FLOWERS	HABITATS	PAGE
Bidens cernua	Nodding Bur-marigold	A	up to 90 cm	Jul–Sep	Damp, ponds, ditches	
Bidens tripartita	Trifid Bur-marigold	A	up to 60 cm	Jul–Sep	Damp, ponds, ditches	
Blackstonia perfoliata	Yellow-wort	A	up to 60 cm	Jun–Oct	Rocky, dunes, grassland	
Blechnum spicant	Hard-fern	P	up to 70 cm	Aug–Nov	Acid soils, rock ledges, shady woods, hedgerows	49
Blysmus compressus	Flat-sedge	P	up to 45 cm	Jun–Jul	Damp, marshes	
Blysmus rufus	Saltmarsh Flat-sedge	P	up to 35 cm	Jun–Jul	Salt marshes	
Bolboschoenus maritimus	Sea Club-rush	P	up to 1.2 cm	Jun–Aug	Coastal, brackish water	
Botrychium lunaria	Moonwort	A	up to 30 cm	Jun–Aug	Dry, mountain ledges, grassland	
Brachypodium pinnatum	Tor-grass	P	up to 1.2 cm	Jun–Aug	Limestone, chalk grassland	
Brachypodium sylvaticum	False Brome	P	up to 100 cm	Jul–Aug	Woodland	
Brassica nigra	Black Mustard	A	up to 90 cm	Jun–Aug	Riversides, cliffs, banks, waste, arable	
Brassica oleracea	Wild Cabbage	Bi/P	up to 90 cm	May–Sep	Sea cliffs	
Briza media	Quaking-grass	P	up to 50 cm	Jun–Aug	Grassland	50
Bromopsis benekenii	Lesser Hairy-brome	P	up to 1.2 cm	Jun–Aug	Limestone, chalk, hedgerows, woods	
Bromopsis erecta	Upright Brome	P	up to 1.2 cm	Jun–Jul	Dry chalky soils	
Bromopsis ramosa	Hairy-brome	P	up to 1.2 cm	Jul–Aug	Common, shady areas, woods	
Bromus commutatus	Meadow Brome	A/Bi	up to 1.2 cm	Jun–Jul	Meadows, waste	
Bromus hordeaceus	Soft-brome	A/Bi	up to 1.2 cm	May–Jul	Dry, grassy, acid, chalky, dunes	
Bromus interruptus	Interrupted Brome	P	up to 15 mm	Jun–Jul	Arable	
Bromus racemosus	Smooth Brome	A/Bi	up to 1.2 cm	May–Jul	Dry, grassy, acid, chalky, dunes	
Bryonia dioica	White Bryony	P	up to 4 m	May–Sep	Scrub, hedgerows, woodland edges	
Bunium bulbocastanum	Great Pignut	P	up to 90 cm	May–Jul	Dry, arable, rough grass	
Bupleurum baldense	Small Hare's-ear	A	up to 30 cm	Jun–Jul	Dry, open banks, near sea	
Bupleurum falcatum	Sickle-leaved Hare's-ear	P	up to 90 cm	Jul–Oct	Waste, hedgerows, grassy areas	
Bupleurum tenuissimum	Slender Hare's-ear	A	up to 60 cm	Jul–Sep	Salt marshes, coastal shingle	
Butomus umbellatus	Flowering-rush	P	up to 1 m	Jul–Aug	Aquatic, freshwater	50
Buxus sempervirens	Box	T	up to 5 m	Apr–May	Dry, hills, open woods	
Cakile maritima	Sea Rocket	A	up to 60 cm	Jun–Sep	Coastal, sandy	
Calamagrostis canescens	Purple Small-reed	P	up to 1.5 m	Jun–Jul	Wet, fens, marshes, woods	
Calamagrostis epigejos	Wood Small-reed	P	up to 2 m	Jun–Aug	Wet, fens, scrub, woods	
Calamagrostis purpurea	Scandinavian Small-reed	P	up to 1.5 m	Jun–Jul	Fens, marshes, woods	
Calamagrostis scotica	Scottish Small-reed	P	up to 100 cm	Jun–Aug	Dry heaths, woods	
Calamagrostis stricta	Narrow Small-reed	P	up to 100 cm	Jun–Jul	Rare, bogs, marshes	
Callitriche brutia	Pedunculate Water-starwort	P	submerged	Apr–Sep	Aquatic, ponds, lakes, streams	
Callitriche hamulata	Intermediate Water-starwort	P	terrestrial	Apr–Sep	Aquatic and acid soils, ditches, streams, ponds	
Callitriche hermaphroditica	Autumnal Water-starwort	P	submerged	May–Sep	Aquatic, streams, rivers, lakes	
Callitriche obtusangula	Blunt-fruited Water-starwort	P	water surface	May–Sep	Aquatic and calcium soils, ditches, streams, ponds	
Callitriche platycarpa	Various-leaved Water-starwort	P	terrestrial	Apr–Sep	Aquatic to terrestrial, mudflats, ditches, ponds, streams	
Callitriche stagnalis	Common Water-starwort	A/P	up to 60 cm	May–Sep	Aquatic, calcium-rich soils, ponds, ditches, streams	
Callitriche truncata	Short-leaved Water-starwort	P	submerged	May–Sep	Aquatic, fertile soils, ditches, ponds	
Calluna vulgaris	Heather	P	up to 80 cm	Jul–Sep	Moors, bogs, roadsides, dunes	38
Caltha palustris	Marsh-marigold	P	up to 30 cm	Mar–Aug	Marshes, fens, ponds, wet woods	50
Calystegia sepium	Hedge Bindweed	P	up to 3 m	Jun–Sep	Coastal, sands, salt marshes, waste	
Calystegia soldanella	Sea Bindweed	P	up to 10 cm	Jun–Aug	Coastal, shingle, sand dunes	
Campanula glomerata	Clustered Bellflower	P	up to 60 cm	Jun–Aug	Grass areas, scrub, waste, open woodland	51
Campanula latifolia	Giant Bellflower	P	up to 90 cm	Jul–Aug	Damp soils, river banks, woods, mountain meadows	
Campanula patula	Spreading Bellflower	Bi/P	up to 60 cm	Jul–Sep	Scrub, hedgerows, waste, grassy, open woodland	
Campanula rotundifolia	Harebell	P	up to 60 cm	Jul–Sep	Dry, acid or chalky, grassy, heaths, downs	51
Campanula trachelium	Nettle-leaved Bellflower	P	up to 90 cm	Jul–Sep	Chalky, hedgerows, scrub, woodland edges	51
Capsella bursa-pastoris	Shepherd's-purse	A	up to 60 cm	Mar–Nov	Common weed, embankments, waste, cultivated land	
Cardamine amara	Large Bitter-cress	P	up to 60 cm	Apr–Jun	Damp, marshes, fens, stream banks, pastures	
Cardamine bulbifera	Coralroot	P	up to 60 cm	May–Jun	Chalky, woodland, stream banks	
Cardamine flexuosa	Wavy Bitter-cress	Bi/P	up to 60 cm	Apr–Sep	Damp, shady areas	
Cardamine hirsuta	Hairy Bitter-cress	A	up to 30 cm	Feb–Nov	Rocky, walls, bare, cult. land	
Cardamine impatiens	Narrow-leaved Bitter-cress	A	up to 60 cm	May–Aug	Chalky, damp, shady, rocky, woods	
Cardamine pratensis	Cuckooflower	P	up to 60 cm	Apr–Jun	Damp pastures, meadows, hedgerows, roadsides	27, 52
Carduus crispus	Welted Thistle	P	up to 2 m	Jun–Aug	Roadsides, waste, grassy	
Carduus nutans	Musk Thistle	Bi	up to 1.5 m	May–Sep	Chalky, grassy, arable, riverbanks, roadsides	
Carduus tenuiflorus	Slender Thistle	A/Bi	up to 90 cm	May–Aug	Dry, waste, roadsides, sea cliffs	
Carex acuta	Slender Tufted-sedge	P	up to 1.2 cm	May–Jun	Freshwater margins, marshes	
Carex acutiformis	Lesser Pond-sedge	P	up to 1.5 m	May–Jun	Marshes, meadows, pond and riversides	
Carex appropinquata	Fibrous Tussock-sedge	P	up to 80 cm	May–Jun	Peaty, marshes, fens, woods	
Carex aquatilis	Water Sedge	P	up to 1.1 m	May–Jun	River edges, swamps, lake shores	
Carex arenaria	Sand Sedge	P	up to 40 cm	May	Coastal, sand dunes	
Carex atrata	Black Alpine-sedge	P	up to 60 cm	May–Jun	Grassy, rocky, mountains	
Carex atrofusca	Scorched Alpine-sedge	P	up to 35 cm	May–Jun	Wet, stony, mountains	
Carex bigelowii	Stiff Sedge	P	up to 30 cm	May–Jun	Stony, mountains, heaths	
Carex binervis	Green-ribbed Sedge	P	up to 1.5 m	May–Jun	Grassy, acid heaths, moors	

BOTANICAL NAME	COMMON NAME	TYPE	MAX. HEIGHT	FLOWERS	HABITATS	PAGE
Carex buxbaumii	Club Sedge	P	up to 80 cm	May–Jun	Wet, grassy, fens	
Carex capillaris	Hair Sedge	P	up to 40 cm	May–Jun	Wet, chalky, woods, hills	
Carex caryophyllea	Spring-sedge	P	up to 30 cm	Apr–May	Dry, chalky, grassy	
Carex chordorrhiza	String Sedge	P	up to 40 cm	May–Jun	Wet, bogs	
Carex curta	White Sedge	P	up to 50 cm	May–Jun	Wet, acid, bogs, heaths, mountains	
Carex davalliana	Davall's Sedge	P	up to 40 cm	May–Jun	Wet, grassy, mountains	
Carex depauperata	Starved Wood-sedge	P	up to 100 cm	May–Jun	Dry, chalky, woods, scrub	
Carex diandra	Lesser Tussock-sedge	P	up to 60 cm	May–Jun	Wet, acid, peaty, meadows	
Carex digitata	Fingered Sedge	P	up to 30 cm	Apr–May	Dry, chalky, grassy, rocks	
Carex dioica	Dioecious Sedge	P	up to 40 cm	May–Jun	Chalky, peaty, marshes	
Carex distans	Distant Sedge	P	up to 100 cm	May–Jun	Damp, marshes, coastal, sandy, rocky	
Carex disticha	Brown Sedge	P	up to 100 cm	May–Jun	Damp, grassy, fens, dune slacks	
Carex divisa	Divided Sedge	P	up to 80 cm	May–Jun	Damp, grassy, marshes, dune slacks	
Carex divulsa	Grey Sedge	P	up to 75 cm	Jun–Oct	Grassy, chalky	
Carex echinata	Star Sedge	P	up to 40 cm	May–Jun	Wet, acid, heaths, bogs, marshes	
Carex elata	Tufted-sedge	P	up to 100 cm	May–Jun	Shallow freshwater, fens, swamps	
Carex elongata	Elongated Sedge	P	up to 80 cm	May–Jun	Damp meadows, alder woods	
Carex ericetorum	Rare Spring-sedge	P	up to 30 cm	Apr–May	Dry, chalky, grassy, heaths	
Carex extensa	Long-bracted Sedge	P	up to 40 cm	May–Jun	Salt marshes, coastal	
Carex filiformis	Downy-fruited Sedge	P	up to 50 cm	May–Jun	Damp, chalky, grassy	
Carex flacca	Glaucous Sedge	P	up to 60 cm	Apr–May	Damp, limestone, chalky, grassy, fens, dunes	
Carex flava	Large Yellow-sedge	P	up to 70 cm	May–Jun	Chalky, fens, marshes	
Carex hirta	Hairy Sedge	P	up to 70 cm	May–Jun	Damp, grassy	
Carex hostiana	Tawny Sedge	P	up to 60 cm	May–Jun	Wet, grassy, marshes, fens, bogs	
Carex humilis	Dwarf Sedge	P	up to 10 cm	Mar–Apr	Dry, chalky, grassy	
Carex lachenalii	Hare's-foot Sedge	P	up to 30 cm	May–Jun	Wet, grassy, marshes, heaths, mountains	
Carex laevigata	Smooth-stalked Sedge	P	up to 1.2 m	May–Jun	Damp, shady, clay, woods,	
Carex lasiocarpa	Slender Sedge	P	up to 1.2 m	May–Jun	Marshes, swamps	
Carex limosa	Bog-sedge	P	up to 40 cm	May–Jun	Peaty bogs, lake margins	
Carex magellanica	Tall Bog-sedge	P	up to 40 cm	May–Jun	Wet, bogs	
Carex maritima	Curved Sedge	P	up to 18 cm	May–Jun	Coastal, sandy	
Carex microglochin	Bristle Sedge	P	up to 12 cm	Jul	Mountain flushes	
Carex montana	Soft-leaved Sedge	P	up to 40 cm	May–Jun	Dry, grassy, chalky, scrub, woods	
Carex muricata	Prickly Sedge	P	up to 100 cm	May–Jun	Acid soils	
Carex nigra	Common Sedge	P	up to 70 cm	May–Jun	Wet, grassy, moors, marshes, dune slacks	
Carex norvegica	Close-headed Alpine-sedge	P	up to 60 cm	Jun–Jul	Damp, grassy, stony, woods	
Carex ornithopoda	Bird's-foot Sedge	P	up to 30 cm	May–Jun	Dry, chalky, grassy, rocky	
Carex otrubae	False Fox-sedge	P	up to 100 cm	May–Jun	Damp, heavy soils, grassy	
Carex ovalis	Oval Sedge	P	up to 60 cm	May–Jun	Damp, acid, grassy, heaths, moors	
Carex pallescens	Pale Sedge	P	up to 60 cm	May–Jun	Damp, clay, grassy	
Carex panicea	Carnation Sedge	P	up to 50 cm	May–Jun	Wet, moors, mires	
Carex paniculata	Greater Tussock-sedge	P	up to 1.5 m	May–Jun	Peaty, fens, marshes, woods	
Carex pauciflora	Few-flowered Sedge	P	up to 25 cm	May–Jun	Wet, peaty, bogs, moors	
Carex pendula	Pendulous Sedge	P	up to 2.4 m	May–Jun	Heavy soils, woods, shady streams	
Carex pilulifera	Pill Sedge	P	up to 30 cm	May–Jun	Dry, grassy, acid heaths, moors	
Carex pseudocyperus	Cyperus Sedge	P	up to 1.2 m	May–Jun	Freshwater swamps	
Carex pulicaris	Flea Sedge	P	up to 30 cm	May–Jun	Damp, chalky, fens	
Carex punctata	Dotted Sedge	P	up to 100 cm	May–Jun	Damp, grassy, rocky, coastal	
Carex rariflora	Mountain Bog-sedge	P	up to 20 cm	May–Jun	Peaty places, mountains	
Carex recta	Estuarine Sedge	P	up to 100 cm	May–Jun	Muddy estuaries	
Carex remota	Remote Sedge	P	up to 60 cm	May–Jun	Damp, shady woods	
Carex riparia	Greater Pond-sedge	P	up to 1.3 m	May–Jun	Marshes, meadows, swamps, ponds, rivers	
Carex rostrata	Bottle Sedge	P	up to 100 cm	May–Jun	Wet, peaty, lake margins, swamps	
Carex rupestris	Rock Sedge	P	up to 20 cm	May–Jun	Dry, stony, rocky, mountain ledges	
Carex saxatilis	Russet Sedge	P	up to 40 cm	May–Jun	Mires, mountains	
Carex spicata	Spiked Sedge	P	up to 100 cm	May–Jun	Grassy, chalky	
Carex strigosa	Thin-spiked Wood-sedge	P	up to 70 cm	May–Jun	Wet, chalky, woods	
Carex sylvatica	Wood-sedge	P	up to 60 cm	May–Jun	Woods	
Carex trinervis	Three-nerved Sedge	P	up to 30 cm	May–Jun	Damp, coastal, sandy, heaths	
Carex vaginata	Sheathed Sedge	P	up to 50 cm	May–Jun	Damp, woods, mountain ledges	
Carex vesicaria	Bladder-sedge	P	up to 1.2 m	May–Jun	Wet, peaty, freshwater lake margins	
Carex viridula	Yellow-sedge	P	up to 30 cm	Jun	Damp, grassy, acid, fens	
Carex vulpina	True Fox-sedge	P	up to 100 cm	May–Jun	Damp, grassy, clay soils	
Carlina vulgaris	Carline Thistle	Bi	up to 30 cm	Jul–Sep	Dry, chalky, grassy, sand dunes	52
Carpinus betulus	Hornbeam	T	up to 25 m	Apr–May	Woods, scrub, hedgerows	
Carum verticillatum	Whorled Caraway	A	up to 90 cm	Jul–Aug	Damp acid soils, marshy meadows, stream beds	
Catabrosa aquatica	Whorl-grass	P	up to 70 cm	May–Jul	Wet, stream and pond edges	
Catapodium marinum	Sea Fern-grass	A	up to 15 cm	May–Jul	Sea, shingle, rocks	

BOTANICAL NAME	COMMON NAME	TYPE	MAX. HEIGHT	FLOWERS	HABITATS	PAGE
Catapodium rigidum	Fern-grass	A	up to 15 cm	May–Jul	Dry, walls, ledges, banks	
Centaurea nigra	Black Knapweed	P	up to 90 cm	Jun–Sep	Pastures, meadows, roadsides, rough grass	28
Centaurea scabiosa	Greater Knapweed	P	up to 90 cm	Jul–Sep	Dry, chalky, roadsides, scrub, rough grass	
Centaurium erythraea	Common Centaury	Bi	up to 30 cm	Jun–Sep	Dry, well-drained soils, scrub, grassy, woodland edges	
Centaurium littorale	Seaside Centaury	Bi	up to 30 cm	Jun–Sep	Dry, scrub, grassy, sea sand dunes	
Centaurium pulchellum	Lesser Centaury	A	up to 30 cm	Jun–Sep	Damp, grassy, close to sea	
Centaurium scilloides	Perennial Centaury	P	up to 30 cm	Jun–Aug	Sea, grassy cliffs	
Centaurium tenuiflorum	Slender Centaury	A	up to 30 cm	Jun–Sep	Damp, coastal, grassy	
Cephalanthera damasonium	White Helleborine	O	up to 60 cm	May–Jul	Chalky, shady, often beech woods	
Cephalanthera longifolia	Narrow-leaved Helleborine	O	up to 60 cm	May–Jun	Chalky, shady	
Cephalanthera rubra	Red Helleborine	O	up to 60 cm	Jun–Jul	Chalky, limestone, often beech woods	
Cerastium alpinum	Alpine Mouse-ear	P	up to 10 cm	Jun–Aug	Mountain, ledges, rocks	
Cerastium arcticum	Arctic Mouse-ear	P	up to 10 cm	Jun–Aug	Mountain, screes, ledges, rocks	
Cerastium arvense	Field Mouse-ear	P	up to 10 cm	Apr–Aug	Dry, chalky, slightly acid, grassy banks, roadsides	
Cerastium cerastoides	Starwort Mouse-ear	P	up to 10 cm	Jun–Aug	Damp, rocky, grassy, mountain screes	
Cerastium diffusum	Sea Mouse-ear	A	up to 30 cm	Mar–Jul	Dry, coastal, stony, grassy	
Cerastium fontanum	Common Mouse-ear	P	up to 30 cm	Apr–Nov	Chalky or neutral soils, grassy, shingle, sand dunes	
Cerastium glomeratum	Sticky Mouse-ear	A	up to 30 cm	Apr–Oct	Common, arable, paths, fields	
Cerastium nigrescens	Shetland Mouse-ear	P	up to 10 cm	Jun–Aug	Mountains	
Cerastium pumilum	Dwarf Mouse-ear	A	up to 12 cm	Apr–Jun	Chalky, dry, grassy	
Cerastium semidecandrum	Little Mouse-ear	A	up to 20 cm	Mar–May	Chalky, dry, sandy	
Ceratocapnos claviculata	Climbing Corydalis	A	up to 90 cm	Jun–Sep	Acid soils, scrub, heaths, woods	
Ceratophyllum demersum	Rigid Hornwort	P	up to 1.2 cm	Jul–Sep	Aquatic, freshwater, slow-moving streams, ponds	
Ceratophyllum submersum	Soft Hornwort	P	submerged	Jul–Sep	Aquatic, ditches, ponds, slow-moving canals and streams	
Ceterach officinarum	Rustyback	P	up to 25 cm	May–Aug	Limestone, wall fissures	
Chaenorhinum minus	Small Toadflax	A	up to 30 cm	May–Oct	All soils	
Chaerophyllum temulum	Rough Chervil	Bi	up to 90 cm	May–Jul	Well-drained soils, semi-shady, rough grass	
Chamaemelum nobile	Chamomile	P	up to 30 cm	Jun–Aug	Light sandy soils, lawns, banks, commons	
Chamerion angustifolium	Rosebay Willowherb	P	up to 90 cm	Jun–Sep	Widespread, all soils	
Chelidonium majus	Greater Celandine	P	up to 90 cm	Apr–Oct	Damp, semi-shady, hedge banks, open woodland	
Chenopodium album	Fat-hen	A	up to 90 cm	Jun–Oct	Abundant, rich fertile soils, arable, waste, farmyards	
Chenopodium chenopodioides	Saltmarsh Goosefoot	A	up to 90 cm	Jul–Sep	Coastal, salt marshes	
Chenopodium ficifolium	Fig-leaved Goosefoot	A	up to 90 cm	Jul–Sep	Rich fertile soils, arable, farmyards, waste	
Chenopodium hybridum	Maple-leaved Goosefoot	A	up to 60 cm	Jul–Oct	Arable, farmyards, waste	
Chenopodium murale	Nettle-leaved Goosefoot	A	up to 90 cm	Jul–Oct	Light well-drained soils, waste, rubbish tips, sand dunes	
Chenopodium polyspermum	Many-seeded Goosefoot	A	up to 90 cm	Jul–Oct	All soils, often arable	
Chenopodium rubrum	Red Goosefoot	A	up to 90 cm	Jul–Oct	Rich fertile soils, often coastal	
Chenopodium urbicum	Upright Goosefoot	A	up to 90 cm	Jul–Sep	Rich fertile soils, arable, farmyards, waste	
Chenopodium vulvaria	Stinking Goosefoot	A	up to 60 cm	Jul–Sep	Coastal, shingle, marshes, inland waste	
Chrysanthemum segetum	Corn Marigold	P	up to 45 cm	Jun–Aug	Acid or neutral sandy soils, waste, arable	30
Chrysosplenium alternifolium	Alternate-leaved Golden-saxifrage	P	up to 30 cm	Apr–Jul	Chalky, damp, shady, marshy	
Chrysosplenium oppositifolium	Opposite-leaved Golden-saxifrage	P	up to 10 cm	Mar–Jul	Damp, acid soils, shady, steam banks	
Cicendia filiformis	Yellow Centaury	A	up to 30 cm	Jun–Oct	Damp, peaty, sandy, often coastal	
Cicerbita alpina	Alpine Blue-sow-thistle	P	up to 2 m	Jul–Sep	Rare, damp mountain, grassy, rocky	
Cichorium intybus	Chicory	P	up to 1 m	Jul–Oct	Chalky, rough grass, fields, waste, roadsides	52
Cicuta virosa	Cowbane	P	up to 1.2 cm	Jul–Aug	Damp, marshes, ditches	
Circaea alpina	Alpine Enchanter's-nightshade	P	up to 30 cm	Jun–Aug	Acid soils, damp, shady, rocky, stream banks	
Circaea lutetiana	Enchanter's-nightshade	P	up to 60 cm	Jun–Aug	Chalky, rich soils, shady, woods, coppices	53
Cirsium acaule	Dwarf Thistle	P	up to 10 cm	Jun–Sep	Dry, chalky, grass, pastures	
Cirsium arvense	Creeping Thistle	P	up to 100 cm	Jun–Sep	All soils, widespread	
Cirsium dissectum	Meadow Thistle	P	up to 80 cm	Jun–Aug	Chalky, peaty, damp, road verges, meadows	
Cirsium eriophorum	Woolly Thistle	Bi	up to 90 cm	Jul–Sep	Dry, chalky, scrub, grassy, road verges, banks	
Cirsium heterophyllum	Melancholy Thistle	P	up to 90 cm	Jul–Sep	Damp, chalky, banks, meadows	
Cirsium palustre	Marsh Thistle	Bi	up to 1.3 m	Jul–Sep	All soils, damp	53
Cirsium tuberosum	Tuberous Thistle	P	up to 90 cm	Jun–Aug	Chalky, grassy, scrub, hills	
Cirsium vulgare	Spear Thistle	Bi	up to 90 cm	Jul–Oct	Fertile, rich soils, grassy	
Cladium mariscus	Great Fen-sedge	P	up to 2.5 m	Jul–Aug	Swamps, fens, lake margins	
Clematis vitalba	Traveller's-joy	P	up to 30 cm	Jul–Sep	Chalky, hedgerows, woodland borders	20, 54
Clinopodium acinos	Basil Thyme	A	up to 30 cm	Jun–Sep	Dry, chalky, arable	
Clinopodium ascendens	Common Calamint	P	up to 1.2 cm	Jul–Sep	Dry, chalky, grassy, hedgerows, scrub	
Clinopodium calamintha	Lesser Calamint	P	up to 90 cm	Jul–Oct	Dry, grassy, banks, hedgerows	
Clinopodium menthifolium	Wood Calamint	P	up to 60 cm	Jul–Oct	Chalky, banks, rocky	
Clinopodium vulgare	Wild Basil	P	up to 60 cm	Jul–Sep	Chalky, dry, grassy banks, hedgerows	21
Cochlearia anglica	English Scurvygrass	Bi/P	up to 30 cm	Apr–Jul	Salt marshes, shingle, sand	
Cochlearia danica	Danish Scurvygrass	A	up to 30 cm	Jan–Sep	Coastal cliffs, banks, walls, rocky, sandy	
Cochlearia micacea	Mountain Scurvygrass	P	up to 20 cm	Jun–Sep	Scottish mountains only	
Cochlearia officinalis	Common Scurvygrass	Bi/P	up to 60 cm	Apr–Aug	Coastal, grassy, cliffs, banks	
Cochlearia pyrenaica	Pyrenean Scurvygrass	Bi/P	up to 60 cm	Jun–Sep	Mountains, rocky	

BOTANICAL NAME	COMMON NAME	TYPE	MAX. HEIGHT	FLOWERS	HABITATS	PAGE
Coeloglossum viride	Frog Orchid	O	up to30 cm	Jun–Aug	Chalky, upland pastures	
Coincya monensis	Isle of Man Cabbage	A	up to 1.2 cm	May–Jun	Sea shores	
Coincya wrightii	Lundy Cabbage	P	up to 60 cm	Jun–Jul	Lundy, North Devon	
Colchicum autumnale	Meadow Saffron	P	up to 30 cm	Aug–Sep	Chalky, damp, grassy	54
Conium maculatum	Hemlock	A	up to1.5 m	Jun–Jul	Damp, heavy soils, grassy meadows, banks	
Conopodium majus	Pignut	P	up to 60 cm	May–Jul	Dry, slightly acid soils, grassy, scrub, heaths	
Convallaria majalis	Lily-of-the-valley	P	up to 30 cm	May–Jun	Dry, scrub, woods, mountain meadows	19, 55
Convolvulus arvensis	Field Bindweed	P	up to 2 m	Jun–Sep	Coastal, waste, cult. land	
Corallorhiza trifida	Coralroot Orchid	O	up to30 cm	Jun–Jul	Damp, peaty, woods (pine or birch), sand dunes	
Cornus sanguinea	Dogwood	T	up to 4 m	Jun–Jul	Chalky, woods, scrub, hedgerows	
Cornus suecica	Dwarf Cornel	P	up to30 cm	Jul–Sep	Acid soils, mountain	55
Coronopus squamatus	Swine-cress	A/Bi	up to 30 cm	Jun–Sep	Waste, bare paths	
Corrigiola litoralis	Strapwort	A	up to 10 cm	Jun–Oct	Wet, sandy, gravel	
Corylus avellana	Hazel	T	up to 6 m	Jan–Mar	Woods, hedges	
Corynephorus canescens	Grey Hair-grass	P	up to 35 cm	Jun–Jul	Rare, coastal, sand dunes	
Cotoneaster integerrimus	Wild Cotoneaster	P	up to 1 m	Apr–Jun	Chalky, dry, screes, rocky hills	
Crambe maritima	Sea-kale	P	up to 90 cm	Jun–Aug	Coastal, cliffs, sandy, shingle	
Crassula aquatica	Pigmyweed	A	up to 10 cm	Jun–Sep	Aquatic, muddy pools	
Crassula tillaea	Mossy Stonecrop	A	up to 10 cm	Jun–Sep	Damp, gravel, sand, paths	
Crataegus laevigata	Midland Hawthorn	T	up to 10 m	May–Jun	Heavy soils, woods, hedgerows, scrub	
Crataegus monogyna	Hawthorn	T	up to 10 m	May–Jun	All soils, widespread	
Crepis biennis	Rough Hawk's-beard	Bi	up to 100 cm	Jun–Jul	Chalky, waste, arable, road verges	
Crepis capillaris	Smooth Hawk's-beard	A	up to 80 cm	Jun–Nov	Grassy, heaths, waste, road verges	
Crepis foetida	Stinking Hawk's-beard	A	up to 60 cm	Jun–Aug	Chalky, shingle, waste	
Crepis mollis	Northern Hawk's-beard	P	up to 60 cm	Jul–Aug	Chalky, damp, shady, woods, mountains	
Crepis paludosa	Marsh Hawk's-beard	P	up to 80 cm	Jul–Sep	Shady, damp, meadows	
Crithmum maritimum	Rock Samphire	P	up to 40 cm	Jun–Oct	Coastal, cliffs, sands, shingle	55
Cruciata laevipes	Crosswort	P	up to 60 cm	Apr–Jun	Chalky, meadows, roadsides	
Cryptogramma crispa	Parsley Fern	P	up to 30 cm	Jun–Aug	Walls, scree	
Cuscuta epithymum	Dodder	A	up to 1 m	Jun–Oct	Parasitic, grassy, heaths	56
Cuscuta europaea	Greater Dodder	A	up to 1 m	Jul–Oct	Parasitic, widespread	
Cynoglossum germanicum	Green Hound's-tongue	Bi	up to 60 cm	May–Jul	Chalky, dry, woodland	
Cynoglossum officinale	Hound's-tongue	Bi	up to 60 cm	May–Aug	Dry, grassy, gravel, sand dunes	56
Cynosurus cristatus	Crested Dog's-tail	P	up to 80 cm	Jun–Aug	All soils, grassy	
Cyperus fuscus	Brown Galingale	A	up to 30 cm	Jul–Sep	Muddy, dried-up ponds	
Cyperus longus	Galingale	P	up to 100 cm	Aug–Sep	Ditches, ponds, marshes	
Cypripedium calceolus	Lady's-slipper	O	up to 50 cm	May–Jul	Chalky, hills, slopes, wood borders	
Cystopteris dickieana	Dickie's Bladder-fern	P	up to 45 cm	Jul–Aug	Rare, sea caves, NE Scotland	
Cystopteris fragilis	Brittle Bladder-fern	P	up to 45 cm	Jul–Aug	Rock crevices	
Cystopteris montana	Mountain Bladder-fern	P	up to 40 cm	Jul–Aug	Rare, damp, rocky	
Cytisus scoparius	Broom	P	up to 2 m	Apr–Jun	All soils, dry, sunny	
Daboecia cantabrica	St Dabeoc's Heath	P	up to 70 cm	May–Oct	Acid soils, rocky, woods, heaths	
Dactylis glomerata	Cock's-foot	P	up to 1.4 m	Jun–Sep	Grassy, waste, road verges, meadows	27
Dactylorhiza fuchsii	Common Spotted-orchid	O	up to 45 cm	Jun–Aug	Chalky, grassy, open woods	22, 26, 57
Dactylorhiza incarnata	Early Marsh-orchid	O	up to 40 cm	May–Jul	Damp, grassy, marshes	
Dactylorhiza lapponica	Lapland Marsh-orchid	O	up to 20 cm	Jun–Jul	Damp, chalky, grassy, fens	
Dactylorhiza maculata	Heath Spotted-orchid	O	up to 60 cm	Jun–Aug	Acid soils, damp, grassy, woods	
Dactylorhiza majalis	Western Marsh-orchid	O	up to 20 cm	May–Jul	Chalky, damp, marshes, meadows, fens	
Dactylorhiza praetermissa	Southern Marsh-orchid	O	up to 60 cm	Jun–Jul	Chalky, rich, damp, marshes, pastures	57
Dactylorhiza purpurella	Northern Marsh-orchid	O	up to 30 cm	Jun–Jul	Damp, rich soils, pastures, fens	57
Dactylorhiza traunsteineri	Narrow-leaved Marsh-orchid	O	up to 45 cm	May–Jun	Chalky, damp, fens	
Damasonium alisma	Starfruit	P	up to 30 cm	Jun–Sep	Aquatic, freshwater habitats	
Danthonia decumbens	Heath-grass	P	up to 60 cm	Jun–Aug	Acid, grassy	
Daphne laureola	Spurge-laurel	P	up to 1 m	Jan–Apr	Dry, chalky, woods, rocky, hedgerows	
Daphne mezereum	Mezereon	P	up to 1.5 m	Feb–May	Chalky, scrub, woods, fields	
Daucus carota	Wild Carrot	A/Bi	up to 90 cm	Jun–Aug	Well-drained soils, grassy, coastal	
Deschampsia cespitosa	Tufted Hair-grass	P	up to 2 m	Jun–Aug	Wet soils, ditches, meadows, moors	
Deschampsia flexuosa	Wavy Hair-grass	P	up to 2 m	Jun–Jul	Sandy, peaty, moors, woodland clearings	58
Deschampsia setacea	Bog Hair-grass	P	up to 1.5 m	Jun–Aug	Bogs	
Dianthus armeria	Deptford Pink	A/Bi	up to 30 cm	Jun–Aug	Dry, chalky, sandy, rocky, grassy	
Dianthus deltoides	Maiden Pink	P	up to 60 cm	Jun–Sep	Chalky, acid, grass banks, rocky	58
Dianthus gratianopolitanus	Cheddar Pink	P	up to 30 cm	May–Jul	Limestone, cliffs, rocks, screes	58
Diapensia lapponica	Diapensia	P	up to 5 cm	May–Jun	Rocky, mountains	
Digitalis purpurea	Foxglove	Bi	up to 1.5 m	Jun–Sep	Acid soils, scrub, woodland, hedgerows	
Diphasiastrum alpinum	Alpine Clubmoss	P	up to 50 cm	Jun–Aug	Mountain, grassland, moors	
Diphasiastrum complanatum	Issler's Clubmoss	P	up to 100 cm	Aug–Sep	Woods, heaths	
Diplotaxis tenuifolia	Perennial Wall-rocket	P	up to 90 cm	May–Sep	Rocky, walls, waste	
Dipsacus fullonum	Wild Teasel	Bi	up to 2 m	Jul–Aug	All soils, widespread	59

BOTANICAL NAME	COMMON NAME	TYPE	MAX. HEIGHT	FLOWERS	HABITATS	PAGE
Dipsacus pilosus	Small Teasel	Bi	up to 1.2 m	Aug–Sep	Chalky, damp, shady	
Draba aizoides	Yellow Whitlowgrass	P	up to 15 cm	Mar–May	Chalky, rocky, cliffs, screes, mountains	
Draba incana	Hoary Whitlowgrass	Bi	up to 30 cm	May–Jul	Limestone, rocky, cliffs, screes, mountains	
Draba muralis	Wall Whitlowgrass	A	up to 30 cm	Apr–Jun	Limestone, rocky, walls	
Draba norvegica	Rock Whitlowgrass	P	up to 30 cm	Jul–Aug	Rocky, mountains, screes	
Drosera intermedia	Oblong-leaved Sundew	P	up to 10 cm	Jun–Aug	Acid, damp, peaty, heaths, bogs	
Drosera longifolia	Great Sundew	P	up to 10 cm	Jul–Aug	Damp, acid, sphagnum bogs	
Drosera rotundifolia	Round-leaved Sundew	P	up to 10 cm	Jun–Aug	Wet, acid, bogs, heaths, moors	59
Dryas octopetala	Mountain Avens	P	up to 6 cm	May–Jul	Chalky, rocky, cliffs	59
Dryopteris aemula	Hay-scented Buckler-fern	P	up to 60 cm	Jul–Sep	Shady, woods, banks	
Dryopteris affinis	Scaly Male-fern	P	up to 60 cm	Jul–Oct	Acid soils, woods	
Dryopteris carthusiana	Narrow Buckler-fern	P	up to 1.2 cm	Jul–Sep	Damp, woods, marshes	
Dryopteris cristata	Crested Buckler-fern	P	up to 90 cm	Jul–Aug	Rare, wet, heaths, bogs	
Dryopteris dilatata	Broad Buckler-fern	P	up to 1.5 m	Jul–Sep	Shady, scrub, woods, hedgerows	
Dryopteris expansa	Northern Buckler-fern	P	up to 60 cm	Jul–Sep	Mountains, rocky	
Dryopteris filix-mas	Male-fern	P	up to 90 cm	Jul–Aug	Common, damp, shady, woods	
Dryopteris oreades	Mountain Male-fern	P	up to 90 cm	Jul–Sep	Dry, mountains, screes, walls	
Dryopteris remota	Scaly Buckler-fern	P	uo to 75 cm	Jul–Sep	Scotland and Ireland only, probably extinct in wild	
Dryopteris submontana	Rigid Buckler-fern	P	up to 60 cm	Jul–Aug	Rare, limestone, crevices	
Echium plantagineum	Purple Viper's-bugloss	A/Bi	up 60 cm	Jun–Aug	Coastal, dry, sandy	
Echium vulgare	Viper's-bugloss	Bi	up to 60 cm	Jun–Sep	Dry, chalky, downs, dunes	60
Elatine hexandra	Six-stamened Waterwort	A/P	up to 30 cm	Jul–Sep	Aquatic, shallow ponds and lakes	
Elatine hydropiper	Eight-stamened Waterwort	A	up to 30 cm	Jul–Aug	Aquatic, lakes, ponds, canals	
Eleocharis acicularis	Needle Spike-rush	P	up to 50 cm	Jun–Oct	Shallow freshwater	
Eleocharis austriaca	Northern Spike-rush	P	up to 60 cm	May–Aug	Rich soils	
Eleocharis multicaulis	Many-stalked Spike-rush	P	up to 30 cm	Jun–Aug	Wet acid, heaths, bogs	
Eleocharis palustris	Common Spike-rush	P	up to 60 cm	Jun–Aug	Wet, meadows, marshes, lake and pond edges	
Eleocharis parvula	Dwarf Spike-rush	P	up to 8 cm	Aug–Sep	Salt lakes, tidal mud	
Eleocharis quinqueflora	Few-flowered Spike-rush	P	up to 30 cm	Jul–Aug	Damp, peaty, fens	
Eleocharis uniglumis	Slender Spike-rush	P	up to 60 cm	May–Jul	Coastal marshes	
Eleogiton fluitans	Floating Club-rush	P	up to 50 cm	May–Jul	Acid waters, submerged	
Elymus caninus	Bearded Couch	P	up to 1.1 m	Jun–Aug	Shady, woods	
Elytrigia atherica	Sea Couch	P	up to 1.2 cm	Jun–Aug	Coastal, sand dunes, salt marshes	
Elytrigia juncea	Sand Couch	P	up to 60 cm	Jun–Aug	Coastal, sand dunes	
Elytrigia repens	Common Couch	P	up to 1.2 cm	Jun–Aug	All soils, widespread	27
Empetrum nigrum	Crowberry	P	up to 45 cm	May–Jun	Dry, peaty, moors, woods (pine, birch)	
Epilobium alsinifolium	Chickweed Willowherb	P	up to 30 cm	Jun–Aug	Damp, rich soils, mountains, stream edges	
Epilobium anagallidifolium	Alpine Willowherb	P	up to 10 cm	Jul–Sep	Damp, acid, mountains, stream edges	
Epilobium hirsutum	Great Willowherb	P	up to 2 m	Jun–Sep	Damp, waste, ditches	
Epilobium lanceolatum	Spear-leaved Willowherb	P	up to 60 cm	Jun–Sep	Waste, banks, rocky, road verges	
Epilobium montanum	Broad-leaved Willowherb	P	up to 60 cm	May–Aug	All soils, widespread	
Epilobium obscurum	Short-fruited Willowherb	P	up to 90 cm	Jul–Aug	Damp, ditches, woods, marshes	
Epilobium palustre	Marsh Willowherb	P	up to 60 cm	Jul–Aug	Wet, bogs, marshes, fens	
Epilobium parviflorum	Hoary Willowherb	P	up to 60 cm	Jul–Aug	Damp, waste, marshes, fens	
Epilobium roseum	Pale Willowherb	P	up to 90 cm	Jun–Aug	Damp, waste, hedgerows, woodland	
Epilobium tetragonum	Square-stalked Willowherb	P	up to 90 cm	Jul–Aug	Damp, waste, ditches, stream edges	
Epipactis atrorubens	Dark-red Helleborine	O	up to 60 cm	Jun–Jul	Chalky, woods, rocky, scrub	
Epipactis helleborine	Broad-leaved Helleborine	O	up to 90 cm	Jul–Sep	Chalky, woods (beech), scrub	60
Epipactis leptochila	Narrow-lipped Helleborine	O	up to 60 cm	Jul–Aug	Chalky, shady woods (beech and conifer)	
Epipactis palustris	Marsh Helleborine	O	up to 60 cm	Jul–Aug	Damp, marshes, fens	60
Epipactis phyllanthes	Green-flowered Helleborine	O	up to 60 cm	Jul–Sep	Chalky, woods, scrub, sand dunes	
Epipactis purpurata	Violet Helleborine	O	up to 60 cm	Aug–Sep	Chalky, woods (beech)	
Epipactis youngiana	Young's Helleborine	O	up to 60 cm	Jul–Sep	Heavy metal polluted soil, NE England and Scotland	
Epipogium aphyllum	Ghost Orchid	O	up to 10 cm	May–Jul	Woods (beech)	
Equisetum arvense	Field Horsetail	P	up to 80 cm	Mar–Jun	Common, fields, waste, road verges	
Equisetum fluviatile	Water Horsetail	P	up to 1.4 m	Jun–Jul	Lakes, riversides, marshes, ponds	
Equisetum hyemale	Rough Horsetail	P	up to 100 cm	Jun–Aug	Wet, shady	
Equisetum palustre	Marsh Horsetail	P	up to 60 cm	May–Jul	Wet, heaths, bogs, meadows	
Equisetum pratense	Shady Horsetail	P	up to 50 cm	May	Damp, grassy, sandy, clay, riverbanks	
Equisetum sylvaticum	Wood Horsetail	P	up to 80 cm	Apr–May	Damp, acid, moors, woods	
Equisetum telmateia	Great Horsetail	P	up to 40 cm	Apr	Damp, shady, heavy soils	
Equisetum variegatum	Variegated Horsetail	P	uo to 80 cm	Mar–Jun	Damp, chalky, mountains	
Erica ciliaris	Dorset Heath	P	up to 80 cm	May–Oct	Acid, wet, scrub, heaths, bogs	
Erica cinerea	Bell Heather	P	up to 75 cm	Jul–Sep	Dry, acid, heaths, moors	61
Erica erigena	Irish Heath	P	up to 2 m	Mar–May	Damp, bogs, moors	
Erica mackaiana	Mackay's Heath	P	up to 80 cm	Aug–Sep	Bogs	
Erica tetralix	Cross-leaved Heath	P	up to 70 cm	Jun–Oct	Acid, wet, moors, heaths, bogs, pine woods	61
Erica vagans	Cornish Heath	P	up to 60 cm	Jul–Sep	Dry, rich soils, heaths, woods	

BOTANICAL NAME	COMMON NAME	TYPE	MAX. HEIGHT	FLOWERS	HABITATS	PAGE
Erigeron acer	Blue Fleabane	A/Bi	up to 60 cm	Jul–Aug	Chalky, dry, grassy	
Erigeron borealis	Alpine Fleabane	P	up to 30 cm	Jul–Aug	Chalky, mountains	
Eriocaulon aquaticum	Pipewort	P	up to 30 cm	Jul–Sep	Shallow freshwater, pools, lakes	
Eriophorum angustifolium	Common Cottongrass	P	up to 60 cm	May–Jun	Wet, acid, fens, bogs	
Eriophorum gracile	Slender Cottongrass	P	up to 60 cm	Apr–May	Wet, acid, bogs, moors	
Eriophorum latifolium	Broad-leaved Cottongrass	P	up to 60 cm	May–Jun	Wet, rich soils	
Eriophorum vaginatum	Hare's-tail Cottongrass	P	up to 50 cm	Apr–May	Wet, peaty, bogs	
Erodium cicutarium	Common Stork's-bill	A/Bi	up to 60 cm	Jun–Sep	Dry, grassy	
Erodium lebelii	Sticky Stork's-bill	A/Bi	up to 30 cm	Jun–Sep	Coastal dunes	
Erodium maritimum	Sea Stork's-bill	A/Bi	up to 10 cm	May–Sep	Dry, coastal, grassy, sand dunes	
Erodium moschatum	Musk Stork's-bill	A/Bi	up to 60 cm	May–Jul	Coastal, waste, cultivated land	
Erophila glabrescens	Glabrous Whitlowgrass	A/Bi	up to 25 cm	Mar–Apr	Open, dry calcareous soil	
Erophila majuscula	Hairy Whitlowgrass	A/Bi	up to 9 cm	Mar–May	Calcareous soils, open dry	
Erophila verna	Common Whitlowgrass	A	up to 10 cm	Mar–May	Dry, rocky, stony, sandy	
Eryngium campestre	Field Eryngo	P	up to 60 cm	Jul–Aug	Dry, grassy, coastal	
Eryngium maritimum	Sea-holly	P	up to 60 cm	Jun–Sep	Coastal, shingle, sandy	
Euonymus europaeus	Spindle	T	up to 6 m	May–Jun	chalky, scrub, woods	
Eupatorium cannabinum	Hemp-agrimony	P	up to 90 cm	Jul–Sep	Damp habitats	62
Euphorbia amygdaloides	Wood Spurge	P	up to 90 cm	Mar–May	Damp, acid, woods, coppices	
Euphorbia cyparissias	Cypress Spurge	P	up to 60 cm	Apr–Jun	Chalky, grassy, rocky, scrub	
Euphorbia exigua	Dwarf Spurge	A	up to 30 cm	Jun–Oct	Chalky, waste, arable	
Euphorbia helioscopia	Sun Spurge	A	up to 60 cm	May–Aug	Waste, arable	
Euphorbia hyberna	Irish Spurge	P	up to 60 cm	Apr–Jul	Shady, woods, stream banks	
Euphorbia lathyris	Caper Spurge	Bi	up to 1.2 cm	Jun–Jul	Waste, woods	
Euphorbia paralias	Sea Spurge	P	up to 60 cm	Jul–Oct	Coastal, shingle, sandy	
Euphorbia peplis	Purple Spurge	A	up to 10 cm	Jul–Sep	Coastal, shingle, sandy	
Euphorbia peplus	Petty Spurge	A	up to 60 cm	Apr–Oct	Waste, arable, cultivated	
Euphorbia platyphyllos	Broad-leaved Spurge	A	up to 90 cm	Jun–Oct	Heavy soils, waste, arable	
Euphorbia portlandica	Portland Spurge	P	up to 30 cm	May–Sep	Coastal, sandy, limestone, cliffs	
Euphrasia officinalis	Eyebright	A	up to 25 cm	Jul–Sep	Rocky, woods, pastures, meadows	62
Exaculum pusillum	Guernsey Centaury	A	up to 10 cm	Jul–Sep	Damp, grassy, sandy	
Fagus sylvatica	Beech	T	up to 30 m	Apr–May	Chalky, sandy, woods	
Fallopia convolvulus	Black bindweed	A	up to 90 cm	Jul–Oct	Waste, arable, road verges	
Fallopia dumetorum	Copse bindweed	A	up to 3 m	Jul–Sep	Chalky, scrub, hedgerows	
Festuca altissima	Wood Fescue	P	up to 1.2 m	May–Jul	Shady, woods	
Festuca arenaria	Rush-leaved Fescue	P	up to 90 cm	Jul–Aug	Sand dunes	
Festuca armoricana	Breton Fescue	P	up to 60 cm	Jun–Jul	Dry, grassy, heaths, moors	
Festuca arundinacea	Tall Fescue	P	up to 2 m	Jun–Aug	All soils	27
Festuca filiformis	Fine-leaved Sheep's-fescue	P	up to 7 mm	May–Jun	Moors, heaths	
Festuca gigantea	Giant Fescue	P	up to 1.5 m	Jul–Aug	Damp woods	
Festuca huonii	Huon's Fescue	P	up to 60 cm	Jun–Jul	Dry, grassy, heaths, moors	
Festuca lemanii	Confused Fescue	P	up to 60 cm	Jun–Jul	Dry, grassy, heaths, moors	
Festuca longifolia	Blue Fescue	P	up to 60 cm	May–Jun	Heaths	
Festuca ovina	Sheep's-fescue	P	up to 60 cm	May–Jul	Poor soils, moors, hills	
Festuca pratensis	Meadow Fescue	P	up to 1.2 cm	Jun–Aug	Grassy meadows	
Festuca rubra	Red Fescue	P	up to 90 cm	May–Jul	Sand dunes, salt marshes, grassy	
Festuca vivipara	Viviparous Sheep's-fescue	P	up to 60 cm	May–Jul	Pastures, moors	
Filago lutescens	Red-tipped Cudweed	A	up to 30 cm	Jul–Aug	Sandy, gravel, fields	
Filago minima	Small Cudweed	A	up to 30 cm	Jun–Sep	Sandy, gravel, waste, heaths, fields	
Filago pyramidata	Broad-leaved Cudweed	A	up to 30 cm	Jul–Aug	Sandy, chalky, arable, road verges	
Filago vulgaris	Common Cudweed	A	up to 30 cm	Jul–Aug	Acid, sandy, grassy, banks	
Filipendula ulmaria	Meadowsweet	P	up to 1.5 m	Jun–Sep	Damp, chalky, acid, marshes, fens, stream edges	63
Filipendula vulgaris	Dropwort	P	up to 90 cm	Jun–Sep	Dry, chalky, grassy, meadows, road verges	63
Fragaria vesca	Wild Strawberry	P	up to 30 cm	Apr–Jul	Dry, chalky, rich soils, grassy habitats	
Frangula alnus	Alder Buckthorn	T	up to 5 m	May–Jun	Damp, heaths, woods, hedges	
Frankenia laevis	Sea-heath	P	up to 30 cm	Jun–Sep	Sandy, shingle, salt marshes	
Fraxinus excelsior	Ash	T	up to 40 m	Apr–May	Chalky, scrub, woods	
Fumaria bastardii	Tall Ramping-fumitory	A	up to 60 cm	Apr–Oct	All soils	
Fumaria capreolata	White Ramping-fumitory	A	up to 90 cm	May–Sep	Arable, waste, scrub, hedges	
Fumaria densiflora	Dense-flowered Fumitory	A	up to 60 cm	Jun–Oct	Sandy, chalky, waste, arable	
Fumaria muralis	Common Ramping-fumitory	A	up to 60 cm	Apr–Oct	Waste, arable, banks	
Fumaria occidentalis	Western Ramping-fumitory	A	up to 60 cm	May–Oct	Waste, arable, walls	
Fumaria officinalis	Common Fumitory	A	up to 30 cm	May–Oct	Acid, chalky, waste, cultivated land	
Fumaria parviflora	Fine-leaved Fumitory	A	up to 30 cm	Jun–Sep	Chalky, arable	
Fumaria purpurea	Purple Ramping-fumitory	A	up to 90 cm	Jul–Oct	Waste, cultivated, hedges	
Fumaria reuteri	Martin's Ramping-fumitory	A	up to 60 cm	May–Oct	Arable	
Fumaria vaillantii	Few-flowered Fumitory	A	up to 30 cm	Jun–Sep	Chalky, arable	
Gagea bohemica	Early Star-of-Bethlehem	P	up to 10 cm	Jan–Mar	Dry, rocky, stony	

BOTANICAL NAME	COMMON NAME	TYPE	MAX. HEIGHT	FLOWERS	HABITATS	PAGE
Gagea lutea	Yellow Star-of-Bethlehem	P	up to 30 cm	Mar–May	Damp, basic soils, grassy, scrub, woods	
Galanthus nivalis	Snowdrop	P	up to 30 cm	Jan–Mar	Damp, hedges, meadows, stream banks, woods	63
Galeopsis angustifolia	Red Hemp-nettle	A	up to 60 cm	Jul–Oct	Arable, waste	
Galeopsis bifida	Bifid Hemp-nettle	A	up to 60 cm	Jul–Oct	Arable, heaths, woods, hedge banks	
Galeopsis segetum	Downy Hemp-nettle	A	up to 60 cm	Jul–Sep	Acid, arable	
Galeopsis speciosa	Large-flowered Hemp-nettle	A	up to 90 cm	Jul–Sep	Peaty, arable	
Galeopsis tetrahit	Common Hemp-nettle	A	up to 60 cm	Jul–Oct	Arable, heaths, woods, hedge banks	
Galium aparine	Cleavers	A	up to 1.2 cm	May–Sep	Scrub, woods, hedge banks	
Galium boreale	Northern Bedstraw	P	up to 30 cm	Jun–Aug	Rocky, screes, shingle, grassy	
Galium constrictum	Slender Marsh-bedstraw	P	up to 60 cm	May–Jul	Pond edges, marshes	
Galium mollugo	Hedge Bedstraw	P	up to 90 cm	Jun–Sep	Rich soils, scrub, meadows, woods	
Galium odoratum	Woodruff	P	up to 30 cm	May–Jun	Chalky, woods	64
Galium palustre	Common Marsh-bedstraw	P	up to 60 cm	Jun–Aug	Damp, wet, aquatic	
Galium parisiense	Wall Bedstraw	A	up to 30 cm	Jun–Jul	Dry, sandy, walls	
Galium pumilum	Slender Bedstraw	P	up to 30 cm	Jun–Jul	Chalky, grassy, open woods	
Galium saxatile	Heath Bedstraw	P	up to 30 cm	Jun–Aug	Dry, acid, scrub, pastures	
Galium spurium	False Cleavers	A	up to 1 m	Jun–Jul	Waste, scrub, hedgerows	
Galium sterneri	Limestone Bedstraw	P	up to 30 cm	Jun–Jul	Limestone, chalky, rocky	
Galium tricornutum	Corn Cleavers	A	up to 60 cm	May–Sep	Chalky, dry, waste, cultivated land	
Galium uliginosum	Fen Bedstraw	P	up to 90 cm	Jun–Aug	Wet, marshes, fens	
Galium verum	Lady's Bedstraw	P	up to 30 cm	Jun–Sep	Grassy, roadsides, hedges, open woods	28
Gastridium ventricosum	Nit-grass	A	up to 60 cm	Jun–Aug	Chalky, grassy, coastal	
Genista anglica	Petty Whin	P	up to 60 cm	Apr–Jun	Damp, heaths	
Genista pilosa	Hairy Greenweed	P	up to 1.5 m	May–Jun	Rocky, heaths, woods	
Genista tinctoria	Dyer's Greenweed	P	up to 1.5 m	Jul–Sep	Grassy, roadsides, banks, woods	64
Gentiana nivalis	Alpine Gentian	A	up to 30 cm	Jun–Aug	Rocky, mountains, meadows, marshes	
Gentiana pneumonanthe	Marsh Gentian	P	up to 30 cm	Jul–Oct	Wet, marshy, peaty, acid heaths	
Gentiana verna	Spring Gentian	P	up to 10 cm	Apr–Jun	Acid to chalky, stony, heaths, meadows	
Gentianella amarella	Autumn Gentian	A/Bi	up to 30 cm	Jun–Oct	Dry, chalky, cliffs, hills, dunes	
Gentianella anglica	Early Gentian	Bi	up to 30 cm	Apr–Jun	Chalky, grassy	
Gentianella campestris	Field Gentian	Bi	up to 30 cm	Jun–Sep	Acid, neutral, grassy, pastures, heaths, dunes	64
Gentianella ciliata	Fringed Gentian	Bi	up to 30 cm	Aug–Oct	Dry, rocky, woods, meadows	
Gentianella germanica	Chiltern Gentian	Bi	up to 30 cm	Aug–Oct	Chalky, grassy, scrub	
Gentianella uliginosa	Dune Gentian	A/Bi	up to 20 cm	Jul–Nov	Damp meadows	
Geranium columbinum	Long-stalked Crane's-bill	A	up to 60 cm	Jun–Aug	Dry, chalky, grassy, scrub, arable	
Geranium dissectum	Cut-leaved Crane's-bill	A	up to 60 cm	May–Aug	Grassy, waste, road verges, hedges	
Geranium lucidum	Shining Crane's-bill	A	up to 30 cm	May–Aug	Chalky, shady, rocky, walls, hedgerows	
Geranium molle	Dove's-foot Crane's-bill	A	up to 30 cm	Apr–Sep	Dry, sandy, chalky, grassy, arable, waste	
Geranium pratense	Meadow Crane's-bill	P	up to 90 cm	Jun–Sep	Chalky, roadsides, meadows, hedges	65
Geranium purpureum	Little-Robin	A/Bi	up to 60 cm	May–Sep	Chalky, coastal, rocky, hedges	
Geranium pusillum	Small-flowered Crane's-bill	A	up to 30 cm	Jun–Sep	Grassy, waste, cultivated	
Geranium pyrenaicum	Hedgerow Crane's-bill	P	up to 60 cm	Jun–Aug	Well-drained, hedgerows, meadows, waste	
Geranium robertianum	Herb-Robert	A/Bi	up to 60 cm	May–Sep	Shady, rocky, woods, banks, shingle	
Geranium rotundifolium	Round-leaved Crane's-bill	A	up to 30 cm	Jun–Aug	Chalky, sandy, hedge banks, walls	
Geranium sanguineum	Bloody Crane's-bill	P	up to 60 cm	Jul–Aug	Grassy, woods, limestone rocks, screes	65
Geranium sylvaticum	Wood Crane's-bill	P	up to 60 cm	Jun–Jul	Rich, chalky, pastures, meadows, hedges	65
Geum rivale	Water Avens	P	up to 30 cm	Apr–Sep	Chalky, damp, shady	66
Geum urbanum	Wood Avens	P	up to 60 cm	May–Sep	Shady, woods	
Gladiolus illyricus	Wild Gladiolus	P	up to 60 cm	Jun–Jul	Scrub, heaths, woods	
Glaucium flavum	Yellow Horned-poppy	Bi	up to 90 cm	Jun–Sep	Coastal, sandy, cliffs, shingle, chalky, waste	66
Glaux maritima	Sea-milkwort	P	up to 10 cm	May–Sep	Coastal, rock crevices, shingle, dry salt marshes	
Glechoma hederacea	Ground-ivy	P	up to 30 cm	Apr–Jun	Shady, woods	
Glyceria declinata	Small Sweet-grass	P	up to 50 cm	Jun–Aug	Freshwater, shallow pond margins	
Glyceria fluitans	Floating Sweet-grass	P	up to 1.2 cm	May–Aug	Freshwater, margins, often floating	
Glyceria maxima	Reed Sweet-grass	P	up to 2 m	Jun–Aug	Freshwater, margins	
Glyceria notata	Plicate Sweet-grass	P	up to 80 cm	Jun–Aug	Freshwater, margins, floating	
Gnaphalium luteoalbum	Jersey Cudweed	A	up to 60 cm	Jun–Aug	Damp, sandy	
Gnaphalium norvegicum	Highland Cudweed	P	up to 30 cm	Jul–Aug	Acid, meadows, stony, woods	
Gnaphalium supinum	Dwarf Cudweed	P	up to 10 cm	Jul–Aug	Acid, rocky, damp, meadows	
Gnaphalium sylvaticum	Heath Cudweed	P	up to 30 cm	Jul–Sep	Acid, sandy, scrub, woods, heaths	
Gnaphalium uliginosum	Marsh Cudweed	A	up to 60 cm	Jul–Sep	Damp, sandy, clay	
Goodyera repens	Creeping Lady's-tresses	P	up to 30 cm	Jul–Aug	Woods (conifers), hills, mountains	
Groenlandia densa	Opposite-leaved Pondweed	P	up to 30 cm	May–Sep	Aquatic, freshwater, streams, ponds	
Gymnadenia conopsea	Fragrant Orchid	O	up to 60 cm	Jun–Jul	Chalky, grassy, scrub, fens	66
Gymnocarpium dryopteris	Oak Fern	P	up to 40 cm	Jul–Aug	Damp, shady, woods, rocky, screes	
Gymnocarpium robertianum	Limestone Fern	P	up to 60 cm	Jul–Aug	Limestone, rocky, screes	
Hammarbya paludosa	Bog Orchid	O	up to 10 cm	Jul–Sep	Acid, wet, sphagnum bogs	
Hedera helix	Ivy	P	up to 30 m	Sep–Nov	Shady, woods, walls, hedgerows	67

BOTANICAL NAME	COMMON NAME	TYPE	MAX. HEIGHT	FLOWERS	HABITATS	PAGE
Helianthemum apenninum	White Rock-rose	P	up to 30 cm	Jun–Sep	Dry, chalky, rocky, banks, meadows	
Helianthemum canum	Hoary Rock-rose	P	up to 30 cm	May–Jul	Dry, limestone, rocky, cliffs, meadows	
Helianthemum nummularium	Common Rock-rose	P	up to 30 cm	Jun–Sep	Dry, chalky, rocky, banks, meadows	67
Helictotrichon pratense	Meadow Oat grass	P	up to 100 cm	May–Jul	Dry, grassy	
Helictotrichon pubescens	Downy Oat-grass	P	up to 100 cm	May–Jul	Chalky, grassy	
Helleborus foetidus	Stinking Hellebore	P	up to 90 cm	Jan–May	Dry, chalky, rocky, woods (beech, yew)	68
Helleborus viridis	Green Hellebore	P	up to 30 cm	Feb–Apr	Chalky, damp, scrub, woods	
Heracleum sphondylium	Hogweed	Bi/P	up to 2.5 m	Apr–Sep	Grassy, banks, woods	68
Herminium monorchis	Musk Orchid	O	up to 30 cm	Jun–Jul	Chalky, grassy	
Herniaria ciliolata	Fringed Rupturewort	P	up to 10 cm	Jun–Aug	Coastal, rocky, grassy	
Herniaria glabra	Smooth Rupturewort	A/P	up to 10 cm	May–Oct	Dry, gravelly, sandy	
Hieracium murorum	Hawkweed	P	up to 60 cm	Jun–Aug	Rocky, grassy, walls	
Hierochloe odorata	Holy-grass	P	up to 60 cm	Mar–Jun	Wet, peaty, grassy, lake and river edges	
Himantoglossum hircinum	Lizard Orchid	O	up to 90 cm	Jun–Jul	Grassy, woods, scrub, road verges	68
Hippocrepis comosa	Horseshoe Vetch	P	up to 10 cm	Apr–Jul	Dry, limestone, chalky, grassy	70
Hippophae rhamnoides	Sea-buckthorn	P	up to 5 m	Mar–May	Coastal cliffs, sand dunes	
Hippuris vulgaris	Mare's-tail	P	up to 60 cm	Jun–Jul	Aquatic, freshwater	
Holcus lanatus	Yorkshire-fog	P	up to 100 cm	May–Aug	Grassy, waste	28
Holcus mollis	Creeping Soft-grass	P	up to 100 cm	Jun–Aug	Acid, shady, hedge banks, woods	
Holosteum umbellatum	Jagged Chickweed	A	up to 30 cm	Mar–May	Dry, sandy, walls	
Honckenya peploides	Sea Sandwort	P	up to 10 cm	May–Aug	Maritime, shingle, sandy	
Hordelymus europaeus	Wood Barley	P	up to 1.1 m	Jun–Jul	Chalky, shady, woods (beech)	
Hordeum marinum	Sea Barley	A	up to 30 cm	Jun–Jul	Maritime, grassy, waste	
Hordeum murinum	Wall Barley	A	up to 50 cm	May–Oct	Waste, waysides, walls	
Hordeum secalinum	Meadow Barley	P	up to 70 cm	Jun–Jul	Heavy soils, grassy, meadows, pastures	
Hornungia petraea	Hutchinsia	A	up to 10 cm	Mar–May	Chalky, sandy, rocky	
Hottonia palustris	Water-violet	P	up to 30 cm	May–Jul	Aquatic, freshwater, lakes, ponds	
Humulus lupulus	Hop	P	up to 6 m	Jul–Sep	Peaty, loamy, scrub walls, hedge banks	
Huperzia selago	Fir Clubmoss	P	up to 10 cm	Jul–Sep	Dry, grassy, moors, heaths, mountains	
Hyacinthoides non-scripta	Bluebell	P	up to 30 cm	Apr–Jun	Woods, heaths	70
Hydrocharis morsus-ranae	Frogbit	P	up to 3 m	Jul–Aug	Aquatic, floating	
Hydrocotyle vulgaris	Marsh Pennywort	P	up to 10 cm	Jun–Aug	Damp, grassy, marshes, bogs, fens	
Hymenophyllum tunbrigense	Tunbridge Filmy fern	P	up to 10 cm	Jun–Jul	Acid, damp, shady, rocky	
Hymenophyllum wilsonii	Wilson's Filmy-fern	P	up to 10 cm	Jun–Jul	Acid, damp, shady, rocky	
Hyoscyamus niger	Henbane	A/Bi	up to 90 cm	May–Sep	Coastal, light soils, waste	
Hypericum androsaemum	Tutsan	P	up to 70 cm	Jun–Aug	Rich soils, damp, shady, decd. woods, hedge banks	71
Hypericum elodes	Marsh St John's-wort	P	up to 30 cm	Jun–Sep	Damp, acid, heaths, bogs, water margins	
Hypericum hirsutum	Hairy St John's-wort	P	up to 1.1 m	Jul–Aug	Chalky, scrub, woods, grassy, banks	
Hypericum humifusum	Trailing St John's-wort	P	up to 20 cm	Jul–Oct	Acid, peaty, scrub, heaths, moors, woods	
Hypericum linariifolium	Toadflax-leaved St John's wort	P	up to 20 cm	Jun–Jul	Dry, acid, rocky	
Hypericum maculatum	Imperforate St John's-wort	P	up to 90 cm	Jun–Sep	Damp, meadows, roadsides, woods	
Hypericum montanum	Pale St John's-wort	P	up to 1.2 cm	Jul–Aug	Chalky, woods, hedgerows	
Hypericum perforatum	Perforate St John's-wort	P	up to 90 cm	May–Sep	Dry, chalky, scrub, fields, woods, banks	
Hypericum pulchrum	Slender St John's-wort	P	up to 90 cm	Jun–Aug	Acid, grassy, heaths, woods	
Hypericum tetrapterum	Square-stalked St John's-wort	P	up to 90 cm	Jun–Sep	Damp, grassy, meadows, water margins	
Hypericum undulatum	Wavy St John's-wort	P	up to 90 cm	Aug–Oct	Acid, damp, marshes, bogs, water margins	
Hypochaeris glabra	Smooth Cat's-ear	A	up to 30 cm	Jun–Oct	Sandy, grassy, sand dunes	
Hypochaeris maculata	Spotted Cat's-ear	P	up to 90 cm	Jun–Jul	Chalky, grassy, woods, quarries	
Hypochaeris radicata	Cat's-ear	P	up to 60 cm	Jun–Sep	Acid, sandy, meadows, pastures, verges	
Iberis amara	Wild Candytuft	A	up to 30 cm	May–Sep	Chalky, dry, woods, hills	
Ilex aquifolium	Holly	T	up to 10 m	Apr–Jun	Scrub, woods, rocky	
Illecebrum verticillatum	Coral-necklace	A	up to 10 cm	Jun–Oct	Damp, sandy, gravelly	
Impatiens noli-tangere	Touch-me-not Balsam	A	up to 1.8 m	Jul–Sep	Damp, shady, woods, stream and river banks	
Inula conyzae	Ploughman's-spikenard	P	up to 1.2 m	Jul–Sep	Dry, chalky, rocky, cliffs, scrub, grassy	
Inula crithmoides	Golden-samphire	P	up to 90 cm	Jul–Sep	Coastal, rocky, shingle, cliffs	
Inula salicina	Irish Fleabane	P	up to 90 cm	Jul–Aug	Limestone, rocky, fens, marshes	
Iris foetidissima	Stinking Iris	P	up to 90 cm	May–Jul	Open woodland	
Iris pseudacorus	Yellow Iris	P	up to 90 cm	Jun–Aug	Freshwater, pond margins	71
Isoetes echinospora	Spring Quillwort	P	submerged	Apr–May	Clear stony lakes	
Isoetes histrix	Land Quillwort	P	up to 30 cm	Apr–May	Sandy, peaty cliff tops, Channel Islands and Cornwall	
Isoetes lacustris	Quillwort	P	up to 30 cm	May–Jul	Submerged aquatic, lakes, pools	
Isolepis cernua	Slender Club-rush	P	up to 30 cm	May–Jul	Coastal	
Isolepis setacea	Bristle Club-rush	P	up to 15 cm	May–Jul	Damp, meadows	
Jasione montana	Sheep's-bit	A/Bi	up to 60 cm	May–Aug	Sandy, grassy, rocky, cliffs, heaths	
Juncus acutiflorus	Sharp-flowered Rush	P	up to 100 cm	Jun–Jul	Acid, wet, grassy, marshes	
Juncus acutus	Sharp Rush	P	up to 1.5 m	Jun–Jul	Coastal dunes	
Juncus alpinoarticulatus	Alpine Rush	P	up to 60 cm	Jun–Jul	Wet, mountains	
Juncus ambiguus	Frog Rush	P	up to 20 cm	May–Sep	Coastal, mud, dunes	

BOTANICAL NAME	COMMON NAME	TYPE	MAX. HEIGHT	FLOWERS	HABITATS	PAGE
Juncus articulatus	Jointed Rush	P	up to 60 cm	Jun–Jul	Wet, acid, marshes, moors	
Juncus balticus	Baltic Rush	P	up to 100 cm	Jun–Jul	Damp, sandy	
Juncus biglumis	Two-flowered Rush	P	up to 20 cm	Jun–Jul	Wet, rich soils, mountains	
Juncus bufonius	Toad Rush	A	up to 50 cm	Jun–Jul	Damp, wet, mud	
Juncus bulbosus	Bulbous Rush	P	up to 100 cm	Jun–Jul	Floating or tufted, acid, bogs, heaths	
Juncus capitatus	Dwarf Rush	A	up to 20 cm	May–Jun	Damp, fens, heaths	
Juncus castaneus	Chestnut Rush	P	up to 30 cm	Jun–Jul	Wet, grassy, mountains	
Juncus compressus	Round-fruited Rush	P	up to 40 cm	Jun–Jul	Damp, marshes, fens, grassland	
Juncus conglomeratus	Compact Rush	P	up to 100 cm	May–Jul	Wet, bogs, pastures, woods	
Juncus effusus	Soft-rush	P	up to 1.5 m	Jun–Aug	Wet, bogs, pastures, woods	
Juncus filiformis	Thread Rush	P	up to 60 cm	Jun–Jul	Damp, wet, fens, lakesides	
Juncus foliosus	Leafy Rush	P	up to 35 cm	May–Sep	Wet, marshes, fields, pond and stream edges	
Juncus gerardii	Saltmarsh Rush	P	up to 40 cm	Jun–Jul	Coastal, salt marshes	
Juncus inflexus	Hard Rush	P	up to 1.2 cm	May–Jul	Heavy soils, damp, grassy	
Juncus maritimus	Sea Rush	P	up to 100 cm	Jun–Jul	Coastal, rocky, salt marshes	
Juncus pygmaeus	Pigmy Rush	A	up to 10 cm	Jun	Damp, sandy, peaty	
Juncus squarrosus	Heath Rush	P	up to 50 cm	May–Jul	Acid, moors, heaths	
Juncus subnodulosus	Blunt-flowered Rush	P	up to 100 cm	Jun–Jul	Wet, fens, marshes	
Juncus trifidus	Three-leaved Rush	P	up to 40 cm	Jun–Jul	Rocky, grassy, mountains	
Juncus triglumis	Three-flowered Rush	P	up to 10 cm	Jun–Jul	Acid, wet, mountains	
Juniperus communis	Juniper	T	up to 6 m	May–Jun	Chalky, moors, scrub, conifer woods	
Kickxia elatine	Sharp-leaved Fluellen	A	up to 30 cm	Jul–Oct	Light soils, arable, cultivated soil	
Kickxia spuria	Round-leaved Fluellen	A	up to 30 cm	Jul–Oct	Light soils, cultivated fields	72
Knautia arvensis	Field Scabious	P/Bi	up to 90 cm	Jul–Sep	Dry, chalky, meadows, woods, hedgerows	72
Kobresia simpliciuscula	False Sedge	P	up to 20 cm	Jun–Jul	Damp, chalky, bare ground	
Koeleria macrantha	Crested Hair-grass	P	up to 40 cm	Jun–Jul	Dry, chalky, grassland	
Koeleria vallesiana	Somerset Hair-grass	P	up to 60 cm	Jun–Aug	Dry, chalky, rocky, grassy	
Koenigia islandica	Iceland-purslane	A	up to 6 cm	Jun–Sep	Damp, bare ground, mountains	
Lactuca saligna	Least Lettuce	A/Bi	up to 90 cm	Jun–Aug	Grassy, waste, coastal shingle	
Lactuca serriola	Prickly Lettuce	A/Bi	up to 1.8 m	Jul–Sep	Sand dunes, waste	
Lactuca virosa	Great Lettuce	A/Bi	up to 2 m	Jul–Sep	Waste, sandy, gravelly, banks	
Lamiastrum galeobdolon	Yellow Archangel	P	up to 60 cm	Apr–Jul	Chalky, shady, woods, scrub	73
Lamium album	White Dead-nettle	P	up to 60 cm	Apr–Nov	Grassy, banks, hedges, waste	73
Lamium amplexicaule	Henbit Dead-nettle	A	up to 30 cm	Mar–Dec	Arable, waste, cultivated	
Lamium confertum	Northern Dead-nettle	A	up to 30 cm	May–Sep	Waste, cultivated	
Lamium hybridum	Cut-leaved Dead-nettle	A	up to 30 cm	Mar–Oct	All soils	
Lamium purpureum	Red Dead-nettle	A	up to 30 cm	Mar–Dec	Waste, cultivated	21, 73
Lapsana communis	Nipplewort	A	up to 90 cm	Jun–Oct	Acid to chalky, waste, woods, hedgerows	
Lathraea squamaria	Toothwort	P	up to 30 cm	Mar–May	Fertile soils, woods, hedges	
Lathyrus aphaca	Yellow Vetchling	A	up to 90 cm	May–Aug	Dry, chalky, grassy, woods, field edges	
Lathyrus japonicus	Sea Pea	P	up to 10 cm	Jun–Aug	Coastal, sand dunes, shingle	
Lathyrus linifolius	Bitter-vetch	P	up to 60 cm	Apr–Jul	Grassy, scrub, woods, banks, acid soils, mountains	
Lathyrus nissolia	Grass Vetchling	A	up to 90 cm	May–Jul	Acid or neutral, grassy, banks, scrub	
Lathyrus palustris	Marsh Pea	P	up to 90 cm	Jun–Jul	Damp, chalky, grassy	
Lathyrus pratensis	Meadow Vetchling	P	up to 1.2 cm	May–Aug	Chalky to acid, grassy, pastures, scrub, woods	
Lathyrus sylvestris	Narrow-leaved Everlasting-pea	P	up to 2 m	Jun–Aug	Scrub, road verges, hedges, woods	74
Lavatera arborea	Tree-mallow	Bi	up to 3 m	Jun–Sep	Rocky, cliffs, waste, hedgerows	74
Lavatera cretica	Smaller Tree-mallow	A/Bi	up to 1.5 m	Apr–Jul	Waste, road verges, quarries	
Leersia oryzoides	Cut-grass	P	up to 100 cm	Aug–Oct	Freshwater margins	
Legousia hybrida	Venus's-looking-glass	A	up to 30 cm	May–Aug	Chalky, sandy, arable, bare ground	
Lemna gibba	Fat Duckweed	P	up to 5 mm	May–Jul	Aquatic, floating, freshwater	
Lemna minor	Common Duckweed	P	up to 5 mm	May–Jul	Aquatic, floating, freshwater	
Lemna trisulca	Ivy-leaved Duckweed	P	up to 15 mm	May–Jul	Aquatic, submerged, freshwater	
Leontodon autumnalis	Autumn Hawkbit	P	up to 60 cm	Jun–Oct	Chalky, grassy, rocky	
Leontodon hispidus	Rough Hawkbit	P	up to 60 cm	Jun–Oct	Chalky, grassy	
Leontodon saxatilis	Lesser Hawkbit	P	up to 30 cm	Jun–Oct	Chalky, sandy, grassy	
Lepidium campestre	Field Pepperwort	A/Bi	up to 60 cm	May–Aug	Arable, waste, banks	
Lepidium heterophyllum	Smith's Pepperwort	P	up to 60 cm	May–Aug	Dry, arable, waste	
Lepidium latifolium	Dittander	P	up to 90 cm	Jun–Aug	Damp, salt marshes, sandy	
Lepidium ruderale	Narrow-leaved Pepperwort	A/Bi	up to 30 cm	May–Jul	Coastal, dry, waste, walls, tips	
Leucanthemum vulgare	Oxeye Daisy	P	up to 90 cm	May–Sep	Chalky, slightly acid, woods, grassy, scrub, banks	
Leucojum aestivum	Summer Snowflake	P	up to 60 cm	Apr–Jun	Wet, marshes, meadows, stream and riverbanks	74
Leucojum vernum	Spring Snowflake	P	up to 30 cm	Feb–Mar	Damp, meadows, woods	
Leymus arenarius	Lyme-grass	P	up to 1.5 m	Jun–Aug	Coastal, sandy	
Ligusticum scoticum	Scots Lovage	P	up to 60 cm	Jul–Aug	Coastal, rocky	
Ligustrum vulgare	Wild Privet	P	up to 3 m	May–Jun	Scrub, hedges, banks, road verges	
Limonium auriculae-ursifolium	Broad-leaved Sea-lavender	P	up to 60 cm	Jun–Sep	Coastal, rocky	
Limonium bellidifolium	Matted Sea-lavender	P	up to 30 cm	Jul–Aug	Coastal, sandy, salt marshes	

BOTANICAL NAME	COMMON NAME	TYPE	MAX. HEIGHT	FLOWERS	HABITATS	PAGE
Limonium binervosum	Rock Sea-lavender	P	up to 30 cm	Jul–Sep	Coastal, cliffs, shingle, rocky	
Limonium humile	Lax-flowered Sea-lavender	P	up to 30 cm	Jul–Aug	Coastal, salt marshes	
Limonium normannicum	Alderney Sea-lavender	P	up to 60 cm	Jun–Sep	Coastal, rocky	
Limonium vulgare	Common Sea-lavender	P	up to 30 cm	Jul–Sep	Muddy salt marshes	
Limosella aquatica	Mudwort	A	up to 10 cm	Jul–Oct	Aquatic, muddy edges of pools	
Limosella australis	Welsh Mudwort	A	up to 10 cm	Jun–Oct	Rare, aquatic, muddy edges of pools	
Linaria pelisseriana	Jersey Toadflax	A	up to 60 cm	May–Jul	Waste, heaths, cultivated	
Linaria repens	Pale Toadflax	P	up to 1.2 m	Jun–Sep	Dry, rocky, waste, cultivated	
Linaria vulgaris	Common Toadflax	P	up to 90 cm	Jul–Oct	Grassy, banks, waste, roadsides	
Linnaea borealis	Twinflower	P	up to 10 cm	Jun–Aug	Heaths, woods (conifers)	
Linum bienne	Pale Flax	Bi/P	up to 60 cm	May–Sep	Dry, chalky, coastal, grassy	
Linum catharticum	Fairy Flax	A	up to 30 cm	May–Sep	Chalky, coastal, grassy, cliffs, heaths	29
Linum perenne	Perennial Flax	P	up to 60 cm	May–Jul	Dry, chalky, grassy	
Liparis loeselii	Fen Orchid	O	up to 30 cm	Jun–Jul	Wet, chalky, fens, bogs, dunes	
Listera cordata	Lesser Twayblade	P	up to 30 cm	Jun–Aug	Moors, bogs, all woods	
Listera ovata	Common Twayblade	P	up to 60 cm	May–Jul	Chalky, marshy, woods	
Lithospermum arvense	Field Gromwell	A	up to 60 cm	Apr–Sep	All soils	
Lithospermum officinale	Common Gromwell	P	up to 90 cm	May–Aug	Scrub, hedge banks, woods	
Lithospermum purpureocaeruleum	Purple Gromwell	P	up to 60 cm	Apr–Jun	Chalky, scrub, woods	
Littorella uniflora	Shoreweed	P	up to 7 cm	Jun–Aug	Aquatic, submerged, maritime, shallow water	
Lloydia serotina	Snowdon Lily	P	up to 15 cm	Jun–Jul	Rocky, mountain, ledges	
Lobelia dortmanna	Water Lobelia	P	up to 60 cm	Jul–Aug	Aquatic, acid, lakes, pools	
Lobelia urens	Heath Lobelia	P	up to 60 cm	Jul–Oct	Grassy, woodland, heaths	
Loiseleuria procumbens	Trailing Azalea	P	up to 30 cm	May–Jul	Dry, peaty, rocky, moors, mountains	
Lolium perenne	Perennial Rye-grass	P	up to 90 cm	May–Nov	Grassy habitats	27
Lonicera periclymenum	Honeysuckle	P	up to 6 m	Jun–Oct	Chalky, acid, woods, scrub, hedgerows, cliffs	75
Lonicera xylosteum	Fly Honeysuckle	P	up to 3 m	May–Jul	Limestone, scrub, woods, hedge banks	
Lotus angustissimus	Slender Bird's-foot-trefoil	A	up to 30 cm	Jul–Aug	Dry, coastal, grassy	
Lotus corniculatus	Common Bird's-foot-trefoil	P	up to 30 cm	Jun–Sep	Grassy, heaths, roadsides	27, 75
Lotus glaber	Narrow-leaved Bird's-foot-trefoil	P	up to 30 cm	Jun–Aug	Chalky, grassy, dunes	
Lotus pedunculatus	Greater Bird's-foot-trefoil	P	up to 60 cm	Jun–Aug	Damp, pastures, ditches, water edges	
Lotus subbiflorus	Hairy Bird's-foot-trefoil	A	up to 30 cm	Jul–Aug	Dry, sandy, grassy, fields, walls, dunes	
Ludwigia palustris	Hampshire-purslane	P	up to 10 cm	Jun–Jul	Wet, shallow pools, stream edges	
Luronium natans	Floating Water-plantain	P	up to 50 cm	May–Aug	Aquatic, floating, streams, ponds	
Luzula arcuata	Curved Wood-rush	P	up to 25 cm	Jun–Jul	Wet, stony, mountains	
Luzula campestris	Field Wood-rush	P	up to 30 cm	Apr–May	Dry, grassland	
Luzula forsteri	Southern Wood-rush	P	up to 30 cm	Mar–May	Shady, woods, banks	
Luzula multiflora	Heath Wood-rush	P	up to 30 cm	May–Jun	Acid, grassy, woods, heaths	
Luzula pallidula	Fen Wood-rush	P	up to 30 cm	May–Jun	Acid, grassy, fens, heaths	
Luzula pilosa	Hairy Wood-rush	P	up to 30 cm	Mar–May	Shady, woods, banks	
Luzula spicata	Spiked Wood-rush	P	up to 25 cm	Jun–Jul	Rocky, grassy, mountains	
Luzula sylvatica	Great Wood-rush	P	up to 80 cm	Apr–Jun	Acid, rocky, woods, moors	
Lychnis alpina	Alpine Catchfly	P	up to 30 cm	Jun–Aug	Mineral-rich soils, meadows, mountains	
Lychnis flos-cuculi	Ragged-Robin	P	up to 90 cm	May–Aug	Damp, peaty, mineral-rich, fens, marshes, meadows	75
Lychnis viscaria	Sticky Catchfly	P	up to 60 cm	May–Aug	Dry, acid, rocky, cliffs	
Lycopodiella inundata	Marsh Clubmoss	P	up to 20 cm	Aug–Sep	Wet, acid, moors, heaths, dunes	
Lycopodium annotinum	Interrupted Clubmoss	P	up to 50 cm	Aug–Sep	Dry, acid, moors, heaths, mountains	
Lycopodium clavatum	Stag's-horn Clubmoss	P	up to 100 cm	Jul–Aug	Heaths, moors, mountains	
Lycopus europaeus	Gypsywort	P	up to 90 cm	Jul–Sep	Wet, marshes, woods, ditches, stream and pool edges	
Lysimachia nemorum	Yellow Pimpernel	P	up to 10 cm	May–Jul	Damp, shady	
Lysimachia nummularia	Creeping-Jenny	P	up to 10 cm	May–Jul	Damp, grassy, woods, hedge banks, stream edges	
Lysimachia thyrsiflora	Tufted Loosestrife	P	up to 60 cm	Jun–Jul	Wet, marshes, fens, bogs, rivers	
Lysimachia vulgaris	Yellow Loosestrife	P	up to 90 cm	Jun–Aug	Damp, chalky, fens, marshes, streams	
Lythrum hyssopifolium	Grass-poly	A	up to 30 cm	Jun–Sep	Flooded ground, pools	
Lythrum portula	Water-purslane	A	up to 10 cm	Jun–Oct	Acid, wet, waste, pool edges	
Lythrum salicaria	Purple-loosestrife	P	up to 1.5 m	Jun–Aug	Freshwater, ditches, marshes, riverbanks	
Maianthemum bifolium	May Lily	P	up to 30 cm	May–Jul	Damp, shady, rich soils	
Malus sylvestris	Crab Apple	T	up to 10 m	May–Jun	Scrub, woods, hedgerows	
Malva moschata	Musk-mallow	P	up to 60 cm	Jul–Aug	Dry, fields, banks	76
Malva neglecta	Dwarf Mallow	A	up to 30 cm	May–Sep	Dry, fields, waste, grassy, coastal	
Malva sylvestris	Common Mallow	Bi	up to 1.5 m	Jun–Sep	Dry, waste, meadows, hedgerows, roadsides	
Marrubium vulgare	White Horehound	P	up to 60 cm	Jun–Sep	Dry, chalky, grassy, waste	
Matricaria recutita	Scented Mayweed	A	up to 60 cm	Jun–Aug	Sandy, loamy, arable, waste, cultivated land	
Matthiola incana	Hoary Stock	P	up to 90 cm	May–Aug	Chalky, coastal, cliffs	76
Matthiola sinuata	Sea Stock	P	up to 40 cm	Jun–Aug	Coastal, cliffs, dunes	
Meconopsis cambrica	Welsh Poppy	P	up to 60 cm	Jun–Aug	Damp, shady, rocky, woods, hedges, walls, stream banks	77
Medicago arabica	Spotted Medick	A	up to 60 cm	Apr–Aug	Well-drained, grassy, waste	
Medicago lupulina	Black Medick	A	up to 10 cm	Apr–Sep	Limestone, grassy, verges	

BOTANICAL NAME	COMMON NAME	TYPE	MAX. HEIGHT	FLOWERS	HABITATS	PAGE
Medicago minima	Bur Medick	A	up to 30 cm	May–Jul	Sand dunes, paths	
Medicago polymorpha	Toothed Medick	A	up to 30 cm	May–Aug	Sandy, short turf, often coastal	
Medicago sativa	Sickle Medick	P	up to 90 cm	Jun–Jul	Road verges, fields	
Melampyrum arvense	Field Cow-wheat	A	up to 60 cm	Jun–Sep	Dry, grassy, rocky	77
Melampyrum cristatum	Crested Cow-wheat	A	up to 60 cm	Jun–Sep	Dry, grassy, rocky	
Melampyrum pratense	Common Cow-wheat	A	up to 60 cm	May–Oct	Scrub, heaths, woods	77
Melampyrum sylvaticum	Small Cow-wheat	A	up to 30 cm	Jun–Aug	Scrub, woods	
Melica nutans	Mountain Melick	P	up to 60 cm	May–Jul	Limestone, shady, woods, rocky, mountains	
Melica uniflora	Wood Melick	P	up to 60 cm	May–Jul	Dry, shady, woods, banks	78
Melittis melissophyllum	Bastard Balm	P	up to 60 cm	May–Jul	Shady, rocky, woods, hedges, roadsides	78
Mentha aquatica	Water Mint	P	up to 90 cm	Jul–Sep	Aquatic, ditches, pools	
Mentha arvensis	Corn Mint	P	up to 60 cm	Jul–Sep	Damp, grassy, woods, arable, ditches	
Mentha pulegium	Pennyroyal	P	up to 30 cm	Jul–Oct	Damp, meadows, lake and pool edges	
Mentha suaveolens	Round-leaved Mint	P	up to 90 cm	Aug–Sep	Wet, grassy, ditches, road verges	
Menyanthes trifoliata	Bogbean	P	up to 30 cm	Apr–Jun	Aquatic or semi-aquatic, pools, fens, bogs	
Mercurialis perennis	Dog's Mercury	P	up to 30 cm	Feb–Apr	Limestone, shady	
Mertensia maritima	Oysterplant	P	up to 30 cm	Jun–Aug	Coastal, sandy, shingle	
Meum athamanticum	Spignel	P	up to 60 cm	Jun–Jul	Limestone, mountains, screes	
Mibora minima	Early Sand-grass	A	up to 15 cm	Feb–May	Coastal, sandy	
Milium effusum	Wood Millet	P	up to 1.8 m	May–Jul	Damp, chalky, woods	
Milium vernale	Early Millet	A	up to 50 cm	Apr–May	Sandy, dunes	
Minuartia hybrida	Fine-leaved Sandwort	A	up to 10 cm	May–Sep	Dry, stony, sandy, arable, waste, walls	
Minuartia recurva	Recurved Sandwort	P	up to 10 cm	Jun–Oct	Acid, grassy, stony	
Minuartia rubella	Mountain Sandwort	P	up to 10 cm	Jul–Aug	Mineral-rich, mountains, rocky, ledges	
Minuartia sedoides	Cyphel	P	up to 10 cm	Jun–Aug	Rocky, mountains, ledges, shingle	
Minuartia stricta	Teesdale Sandwort	P	up to 10 cm	Jun–Jul	Wet, rocky, mountains, screes	
Minuartia verna	Spring Sandwort	P	up to 30 cm	May–Sep	Dry, chalky, rocky, screes	
Misopates orontium	Lesser Snapdragon	A	up to 30 cm	Jul–Oct	Arable, waste, road verges, cultivated land	
Moehringia trinervia	Three-nerved Sandwort	A	up to 30 cm	May–Jun	Acid, neutral, shady, woods	
Moenchia erecta	Upright Chickweed	A	up to 10 cm	Apr–Jun	Sandy, gravelly	
Molinia caerulea	Purple Moor-grass	P	up to 90 cm	Jul–Sep	Wet, heaths, moors, fens, marshes	
Moneses uniflora	One-flowered Wintergreen	P	up to 30 cm	May–Aug	Acid, woods (conifers)	
Monotropa hypopitys	Yellow Bird's-nest	P	up to 30 cm	Jun–Sep	Damp, woods (beech, conifers)	
Montia fontana	Blinks	A/P	up to 30 cm	Apr–Oct	Wet, acid, pastures	
Muscari neglectum	Grape-hyacinth	P	up to 30 cm	Mar–May	Dry, grassy, cultivated	
Mycelis muralis	Wall Lettuce	P	up to 90 cm	Jul–Sep	Chalky, rich soils, rocky, walls, waste, woods	
Myosotis alpestris	Alpine Forget-me-not	P	up to 30 cm	May–Sep	Damp, meadows, woods	
Myosotis arvensis	Field Forget-me-not	A/Bi	up to 30 cm	Apr–Oct	Dry, arable, dunes	
Myosotis discolor	Changing Forget-me-not	A	up to 30 cm	May–Sep	Light soils, grassy, woods	
Myosotis laxa	Tufted Forget-me-not	A/Bi	up to 60 cm	May–Sep	Wet, stony, grassy, marshes, stream and pond edges	
Myosotis ramosissima	Early Forget-me-not	A	up to 30 cm	Apr–Jun	Dry, all soils	
Myosotis scorpioides	Water Forget-me-not	P	up to 60 cm	May–Sep	Wet habitats	
Myosotis secunda	Creeping Forget-me-not	A/Bi	up to 30 cm	May–Aug	Wet, acid, peaty	
Myosotis sicula	Jersey Forget-me-not	A/Bi	up to 30 cm	May–Jun	Damp, coastal, dunes	
Myosotis stolonifera	Pale Forget-me-not	A/Bi	up to 20 cm	Jun–Jul	Wet, hills, stream edges	
Myosotis sylvatica	Wood Forget-me-not	Bi/P	up to 60 cm	Apr–Jun	Damp, woods, grassy, mountains	
Myosoton aquaticum	Water Chickweed	P	up to 60 cm	Jun–Aug	Aquatic, fens, marshes, pond and river edges	
Myosurus minimus	Mousetail	A	up to 30 cm	Mar–Jun	Arable, waste, paths	
Myrica gale	Bog-myrtle	T	up to 2.5 m	Apr–May	Wet, heaths, bogs	
Myriophyllum alterniflorum	Alternate Water-milfoil	P	up to 1.2 m	Jun–Jul	Aquatic, peaty, freshwater	
Myriophyllum spicatum	Spiked Water-milfoil	P	up to 2.5 m	Jun–Jul	Aquatic, freshwater, ponds	
Myriophyllum verticillatum	Whorled Water-milfoil	P	up to 3 m	Jul–Aug	Aquatic, freshwater, ponds	
Najas flexilis	Slender Naiad	P	up to 30 cm	Aug–Sep	Aquatic, submerged, lakes, ponds	
Najas marina	Holly-leaved Naiad	P	up to 25 cm	Jul–Sep	Aquatic, freshwater, submerged	
Narcissus pseudonarcissus	Wild Daffodil	P	up to 60 cm	Feb–Apr	Waste, meadows, woods, hills, mountains	33
Nardus stricta	Mat-grass	P	up to 20 cm	Jun–Aug	Sandy, peaty, heaths, moors	
Narthecium ossifragum	Bog Asphodel	P	up to 60 cm	Jul–Sep	Wet, acid, bogs, heaths, moors	
Neotinea maculata	Dense-flowered Orchid	O	up to 30 cm	Jun–Jul	Chalky, grassy, dunes, woods	
Neottia nidus-avis	Bird's-nest Orchid	O	up to 60 cm	May–Jul	Woods, esp. beech woods	
Nepeta cataria	Cat-mint	P	up to 90 cm	Jun–Sep	Chalky, rocky, banks, hedges	
Nuphar lutea	Yellow Water-lily	P	floating	Jun–Sep	Aquatic, freshwater, ponds, streams, rivers	
Nuphar pumila	Least Water-lily	P	floating	Jun–Jul	Aquatic, shallow lakes, pools	
Nymphaea alba	White Water-lily	P	floating	Jun–Sep	Aquatic, freshwater, lakes, ponds, ditches	
Nymphoides peltata	Fringed Water-lily	P	up to 10 cm	Jul–Sep	Aquatic, freshwater, lakes, ponds, ditches	
Odontites vernus	Red Bartsia	A	up to 30 cm	Jul–Oct	All soils	
Oenanthe aquatica	Fine-leaved Water-dropwort	P/Bi	up to 1.5 m	Jun–Sep	Fertile soils, shallow freshwater	
Oenanthe crocata	Hemlock Water-dropwort	P	up to 1.5 m	Jun–Aug	Acid, wet, grassy, woods, pond and stream edges	
Oenanthe fistulosa	Tubular Water-dropwort	P	up to 90 cm	Jun–Sep	Fertile soils, shallow water, marshes	

Complete List

BOTANICAL NAME	COMMON NAME	TYPE	MAX. HEIGHT	FLOWERS	HABITATS	PAGE
Oenanthe fluviatilis	River Water-dropwort	P	up to 1.2 cm	Jul–Sep	Ponds, streams	
Oenanthe lachenalii	Parsley Water-dropwort	P	up to 90 cm	Jun–Sep	Coastal, wet, grassland	
Oenanthe pimpinelloides	Corky-fruited Water-dropwort	P	up to 90 cm	Jun–Jul	Water meadows	
Oenanthe silaifolia	Narrow-leaved Water-dropwort	P	up to 90 cm	Jun–Jul	Water meadows	
Oenothera cambrica	Small-flowered Evening-primrose	A/Bi	up to 90 cm	Jun–Sep	Coastal, dunes, waste	
Oenothera fallax	Intermediate Evening-primrose	A/Bi	up to 90 cm	Jun–Sep	Waste, dunes, banks	
Onobrychis viciifolia	Sainfoin	P	up to 90 cm	Jun–Sep	Chalky, grassy, waste, arable	79
Ononis reclinata	Small Restharrow	A	up to 10 cm	May–Jun	Coastal, sandy, cliffs, grassy	
Ononis repens	Common Restharrow	P	up to 60 cm	Jun–Sep	Chalky, dry, grassy	79
Ononis spinosa	Spiny Restharrow	P	up to 90 cm	Jun–Sep	Chalky, grassy, rocky	
Onopordum acanthium	Cotton Thistle	Bi	up to 3 m	Jul–Sep	Acid, chalky, waste, hedges, cultivated land	
Ophioglossum azoricum	Small Adder's-tongue	P	up to 8 cm	Jul–Aug	Coastal, damp, bare ground	
Ophioglossum lusitanicum	Least Adder's-tongue	P	up to 1 cm	Apr	Coastal, damp, bare ground	
Ophioglossum vulgatum	Adder's-tongue	P	up to 30 cm	Jun–Aug	Damp, chalky, grassy	
Ophrys apifera	Bee Orchid	O	up to 60 cm	Jun–Jul	Chalky, grassy, meadows, sand dunes, quarries	81
Ophrys fuciflora	Late Spider-orchid	O	up to 50 cm	Jun–Jul	Chalky, grassy, fields, road verges	
Ophrys insectifera	Fly Orchid	O	up to 60 cm	May–Jun	Chalky, shady, grassy, scrub, woods	
Ophrys sphegodes	Early Spider-orchid	O	up to 60 cm	Apr–Jun	Chalky, grassy, rocky, banks	
Orchis laxiflora	Loose-flowered Orchid	O	up to 90 cm	May–Jun	Damp, marshes, meadows	
Orchis mascula	Early-purple Orchid	O	up to 60 cm	Apr–Jun	Grassy, scrub, roadsides, woods (beech, oak)	22, 80
Orchis militaris	Military Orchid	O	up to 60 cm	May–Jun	Chalky, grassy, scrub, woods	80
Orchis morio	Green-winged Orchid	O	up to 60 cm	May–Jun	Grassy, scrub, quarries	
Orchis purpurea	Lady Orchid	O	up to 90 cm	May–Jun	Chalky, grassy, scrub, woods, roadsides	81
Orchis simia	Monkey Orchid	O	up to 60 cm	May–Jun	Chalky, grassy, scrub, woods	80
Orchis ustulata	Burnt Orchid	O	up to 30 cm	May–Jun	Chalky, grassy, hills, mountains	81
Oreopteris limbosperma	Lemon-scented Fern	P	up to 90 cm	Aug–Sep	Acid, woods, screes, heaths, stream banks	
Origanum vulgare	Wild Marjoram	P	up to 90 cm	Jul–Sep	Chalky, grassy, scrub, banks	82
Ornithogalum angustifolium	Star-of-Bethlehem	P	up to 30 cm	Apr–Jun	All soils	19
Ornithogalum pyrenaicum	Spiked Star-of-Bethlehem	P	up to 90 cm	May–Jul	Grassy, scrub, woods	12
Ornithopus perpusillus	Bird's-foot	A	up to 10 cm	May–Aug	Dry, acid, gravelly, sandy	
Ornithopus pinnatus	Orange Bird's-foot	A	up to 60 cm	Apr–Oct	Grassy, open areas	
Orobanche alba	Thyme Broomrape	P	up to 30 cm	Jun–Aug	Chalky, rocky, woods	
Orobanche artemisiae-campestris	Oxtongue Broomrape	P	up to 60 cm	Jun–Jul	Grassy, rocky	
Orobanche caryophyllacea	Bedstraw Broomrape	P	up to 60 cm	Jun–Jul	Rough grass, woods	
Orobanche elatior	Knapweed Broomrape	P	up to 60 cm	Jun–Jul	Dry, grassy	
Orobanche hederae	Ivy Broomrape	P	up to 60 cm	Jun–Jul	Walls, woods, hedges	82
Orobanche minor	Common Broomrape	P	up to 60 cm	Jun–Sep	Meadows, cultivated land	
Orobanche purpurea	Yarrow Broomrape	P	up to 60 cm	Jun–Jul	Rough grass	
Orobanche rapum-genistae	Greater Broomrape	P	up to 90 cm	May–Jul	Rough grass	
Orobanche reticulata	Thistle Broomrape	P	up to 30 cm	Jun–Aug	Rough grass, fields	
Orthilia secunda	Serrated Wintergreen	P	up to 30 cm	Jun–Aug	Damp, woods, rocky, mountains	
Osmunda regalis	Royal Fern	P	up to 3 m	Jun–Aug	Wet, shady, acid	83
Otanthus maritimus	Cottonweed	P	up to 30 cm	Aug–Oct	Coastal, sandy, shingle	
Oxalis acetosella	Wood-sorrel	P	up to 10 cm	Apr–Jun	Shady, humus-rich, woods, hedge banks	83
Oxyria digyna	Mountain Sorrel	P	up to 30 cm	Jun–Aug	Damp, rocky, mountains	
Oxytropis campestris	Yellow Oxytropis	P	up to 30 cm	Jun–Jul	Chalky, grassy, rocky, mountains	
Oxytropis halleri	Purple Oxytropis	P	up to 10 cm	Jul–Aug	Dry, acid, grassy, cliffs, mountains	
Papaver argemone	Prickly Poppy	A	up to 60 cm	May–Jul	Dry, sandy, arable, road verges	
Papaver dubium	Long-headed Poppy	A	up to 60 cm	Jun–Aug	All soils	
Papaver hybridum	Rough Poppy	A	up to 60 cm	Jun–Aug	Chalky, arable, road verges	
Papaver rhoeas	Common Poppy	A	up to 60 cm	Jun–Oct	All soils	15, 30
Parapholis incurva	Curved Hard-grass	A	up to 15 cm	Jun–Aug	Grassy, salt marshes, coastal	
Parapholis strigosa	Hard-grass	A	up to 40 cm	Jun–Aug	Grassy, salt marshes, coastal	
Parentucellia viscosa	Yellow Bartsia	A	up to 60 cm	Jun–Sep	Coastal, damp, grassy	
Parietaria judaica	Pellitory-of-the-wall	P	up to 60 cm	Jun–Oct	Dry, well-drained, walls, stony, hedges	
Paris quadrifolia	Herb-paris	P	up to 30 cm	May–Jun	Chalky, damp, shady, woods	
Parnassia palustris	Grass-of-Parnassus	P	up to 60 cm	Jun–Sep	Damp, marshes, fens, moors	
Pastinaca sativa	Wild Parsnip	Bi	up to 90 cm	Jul–Aug	Dry, chalky, grassy	
Pedicularis palustris	Marsh Lousewort	Bi/A	up to 60 cm	May–Sep	Damp, acid, meadows, fens, marshes	
Pedicularis sylvatica	Lousewort	Bi/P	up to 30 cm	Apr–Jul	Damp, peaty, moors, heaths, marshes, bogs	
Persicaria amphibia	Amphibious Bistort	P	up to 60 cm	Jun–Sep	Aquatic and terrestrial, ponds, canals, ditches	
Persicaria bistorta	Common Bistort	P	up to 60 cm	Jun–Oct	Damp, meadows, woods, roadsides	
Persicaria hydropiper	Water-pepper	A	up to 90 cm	Jun–Sep	Damp, acid, meadows, shallow water	
Persicaria lapathifolia	Pale Persicaria	A	up to 90 cm	Jun–Oct	Damp, waste, cult. pond and river edges	
Persicaria laxiflora	Tasteless Water-pepper	A	up to 60 cm	Jul–Sep	Damp, ditches, pond and river edges	
Persicaria maculosa	Redshank	A	up to 60 cm	Jun–Oct	Damp, waste, river, stream, canal banks	
Persicaria minor	Small Water-pepper	A	up to 30 cm	Jul–Sep	Damp, marshes, lake, pond, river edges	
Persicaria vivipara	Alpine Bistort	P	up to 30 cm	Jun–Aug	Damp, grassy, rocky, screes	

BOTANICAL NAME	COMMON NAME	TYPE	MAX. HEIGHT	FLOWERS	HABITATS	PAGE
Petasites hybridus	Butterbur	P	up to 90 cm	Mar–May	Damp, meadows, roadsides, river and steam banks	83
Petrorhagia nanteuilii	Childing Pink	A	up to 60 cm	Jul–Aug	Coastal, sandy, gravelly	
Petrorhagia prolifera	Proliferous Pink	A	up to 60 cm	May–Sep	Dry, chalky	
Petroselinum segetum	Corn Parsley	Bi/A	up to 90 cm	Aug–Oct	All soils	
Peucedanum officinale	Hog's Fennel	P	up to 2 m	Jul–Sep	Coastal, grassy, cliffs	
Peucedanum palustre	Milk-parsley	Bi	up to 1.5 m	Jul–Sep	Wet, chalky	
Phalaris arundinacea	Reed Canary-grass	P	up to 2 m	Jun–Aug	Damp, woods, fens, meadows	
Phegopteris connectilis	Beech Fern	P	up to 30 cm	Jul–Sep	Acid, chalky, shady, woods	
Phleum alpinum	Alpine Cat's-tail	P	up to 50 cm	Jul–Aug	Wet, grassy, rocky, ledges, mountains	
Phleum arenarium	Sand Cat's-tail	A	up to 35 cm	May–Jun	Coastal, sandy, shingle	
Phleum bertolonii	Smaller Cat's-tail	P	up to 70 cm	Jun–Aug	Chalky, grassy	
Phleum phleoides	Purple-stem Cat's-tail	P	up to 90 cm	Jun–Aug	Dry, chalky, sandy, grassy	
Phleum pratense	Timothy	P	up to 1.5 m	Jun–Aug	Grassy, waste	
Phragmites australis	Common Reed	P	up to 3.5 m	Aug–Oct	Freshwater, fens, marshes, swamps	
Phyllitis scolopendrium	Hart's-tongue	P	up to 60 cm	Aug–Mar	Walls, rocky, hedge banks	
Phyllodoce caerulea	Blue Heath	P	up to 35 cm	Jun–Aug	Acid, rocky, heaths, moors, mountains	
Physospermum cornubiense	Bladderseed	P	up to 90 cm	Jul–Aug	Scrub, arable, woods, hedges	
Phyteuma orbiculare	Round-headed Rampion	P	up to 60 cm	Jun–Aug	Dry, chalky, grassy, rocky	84
Phyteuma spicatum	Spiked Rampion	P	up to 90 cm	Jun–Aug	Acid, woods, meadows, road verges	
Picris echioides	Bristly Oxtongue	A/Bi	up to 90 cm	Jun–Nov	Chalky, grassy, waste, stream banks	
Picris hieracioides	Hawkweed Oxtongue	Bi/P	up to 90 cm	Jul–Oct	Dry, chalky, grassy	
Pilosella flagellaris	Shetland Mouse-ear-hawkweed	P	up to 40 cm	Jun–Sep	Grassland	
Pilosella officinarum	Mouse-ear-hawkweed	P	up to 30 cm	May–Sep	Dry, acid, chalky, grassy, banks, walls	
Pilosella peleteriana	Shaggy Mouse-ear-hawkweed	P	up to 40 cm	Jun– Sep	Short well-drained grassland	
Pilularia globulifera	Pillwort	P	up to 10 cm	Jun–Sep	Acid, semi-aquatic, marshes, wet heaths	
Pimpinella major	Greater Burnet-saxifrage	P	up to 90 cm	Jun–Aug	Dry, chalky, grassy, hedges, verges, woods	
Pimpinella saxifraga	Burnet-saxifrage	P	up to 1 m	Jun–Sep	Chalky, rough grass, rocky	
Pinguicula alpina	Alpine Butterwort	P	up to 7 cm	Jun–Aug	Wet, acid, heaths, bogs, ditches, mountains	
Pinguicula grandiflora	Large-flowered Butterwort	P	up to 30 cm	May–Jul	Wet, acid, rocky, bogs	
Pinguicula lusitanica	Pale Butterwort	P	up to 10 cm	Jun–Oct	Wet, acid, heaths, bogs, ditches	
Pinguicula vulgaris	Common Butterwort	P	up to 10 cm	May–Jul	Wet, heaths, bogs, rocky, ditches	
Pinus sylvestris	Scots Pine	T	up to 40 m	May–Jun	Woods, forests, heaths, moors	
Plantago coronopus	Buck's-horn Plantain	Bi/P	up to 10 cm	May–Jul	Coastal, sandy, gravelly	
Plantago lanceolata	Ribwort Plantain	P	up to 60 cm	Apr–Oct	All soils	
Plantago major	Greater Plantain	P	up to 30 cm	Jun–Oct	Grassy, waste	
Plantago maritima	Sea Plantain	P	up to 30 cm	Jun–Aug	Coastal, chalky	
Plantago media	Hoary Plantain	P	up to 60 cm	May–Aug	Dry, chalky, grassy, waste	84
Platanthera bifolia	Lesser Butterfly-orchid	O	up to 40 cm	Jun–Jul	Chalky, woods, meadows, heaths, marshy	
Platanthera chlorantha	Greater Butterfly-orchid	O	up to 45 cm	Jun–Jul	Chalky, damp, woods, heaths, meadows	
Poa alpina	Alpine Meadow-grass	P	up to 30 cm	Jun–Aug	Grassy, rocky, mountains	
Poa angustifolia	Narrow-leaved Meadow-grass	P	up to 50 cm	Apr–Jun	Lime-rich, grassland	
Poa annua	Annual Meadow-grass	A	up to 30 cm	Jan–Dec	Bare disturbed ground	
Poa bulbosa	Bulbous Meadow-grass	P	up to 40 cm	Mar–May	Coastal, dry, sandy	
Poa compressa	Flattened Meadow-grass	P	up to 40 cm	Jun–Aug	Dry, rocky, waste, walls	
Poa flexuosa	Wavy Meadow-grass	P	up to 20 cm	Jul–Aug	Rocky, mountains, screes	
Poa glauca	Glaucous Meadow-grass	P	up to 35 cm	Jul–Aug	Rocky, mountains, screes	
Poa humilis	Spreading Meadow-grass	P	up to 60 cm	May–Jul	Damp, grassy	
Poa infirma	Early Meadow-grass	A	up to 30 cm	Mar–May	Coastal, sandy	
Poa nemoralis	Wood Meadow-grass	P	up to 70 cm	May–Jul	Shady, woods	
Poa pratensis	Smooth Meadow-grass	P	up to 50 cm	Apr–Jun	Dry, grassy, walls	
Poa trivialis	Rough Meadow-grass	P	up to 90 cm	May–Jul	Damp, shady, grassy	
Polemonium caeruleum	Jacob's-ladder	P	up to 90 cm	May–Aug	Damp, limestone, rocky, meadows	85
Polycarpon tetraphyllum	Four-leaved Allseed	A	up to 10 cm	Jun–Aug	Sandy, rocky, bare ground	
Polygala amarella	Dwarf Milkwort	P	up to 30 cm	May–Aug	Damp, chalky, limestone, grassy	
Polygala calcarea	Chalk Milkwort	P	up to 30 cm	May–Jun	Chalky grassland	
Polygala serpyllifolia	Heath Milkwort	P	up to 30 cm	May–Aug	Acid, grassy, heaths	
Polygala vulgaris	Common Milkwort	P	up to 30 cm	May–Sep	Chalky, limestone, heaths, dunes	85
Polygonatum multiflorum	Solomon's-seal	P	up to 90 cm	May–Jun	Chalky, woods, scrub	85
Polygonatum odoratum	Angular Solomon's-seal	P	up to 30 cm	May–Jun	Chalky, rocky, woods	
Polygonatum verticillatum	Whorled Solomon's-seal	P	up to 90 cm	Jun–Jul	Rocky, scrub, woods, mountains	
Polygonum arenastrum	Equal-leaved Knotgrass	A	up to 10 cm	Jul–Sep	Waste, road verges, cultivated land	
Polygonum aviculare	Knotgrass	A	up to 60 cm	Jun–Nov	Waste, roadsides, seashores	
Polygonum boreale	Northern Knotgrass	A	up to 20 cm	Jun–Nov	Seashores, waste	
Polygonum maritimum	Sea Knotgrass	P	up to 60 cm	Jul–Sep	Coastal, sandy, shingle, rocky	
Polygonum oxyspermum	Ray's Knotgrass	A/Bi	up to 10 cm	Jun–Nov	Coastal, sandy, shingle	
Polygonum rurivagum	Cornfield Knotgrass	A	up to 60 cm	Jun–Oct	Dry, chalky, arable	
Polypodium cambricum	Southern Polypody	P	up to 50 cm	Dec–May	Basic soils, walls	
Polypodium interjectum	Intermediate Polypody	P	up to 50 cm	Sep–Feb	Basic soils, damp, coastal	

BOTANICAL NAME	COMMON NAME	TYPE	MAX. HEIGHT	FLOWERS	HABITATS	PAGE
Polypodium vulgare	Polypody	P	up to 50 cm	Aug–Mar	Acid soils, walls, rocks	
Polypogon monspeliensis	Annual Beard-grass	A	up to 90 cm	Jun–Aug	Coastal, grassy	
Polystichum aculeatum	Hard Shield-fern	P	up to 90 cm	Jul–Feb	Rocky, hedges, woods, hills	
Polystichum lonchitis	Holly-fern	P	up to 60 cm	Aug–Apr	Chalky, rocky, hills	
Polystichum setiferum	Soft Shield-fern	P	up to 1.5 m	Jul–Jan	Wet, woods, rocky, banks	
Populus nigra	Black-poplar	T	up to 30 m	Mar–Apr	Freshwater, wet woods, river valleys	
Populus tremula	Aspen	T	up to 20 m	Feb–Mar	Damp, moors, fens, woods	
Potamogeton acutifolius	Sharp-leaved Pondweed	P	floating	Jun–Sep	Chalky water, lakes, streams, ponds	
Potamogeton alpinus	Red Pondweed	P	floating	Jun–Aug	Rich organic waters	
Potamogeton berchtoldii	Small Pondweed	P	floating	Jun–Sep	Acid waters, ditches, ponds, lakes	
Potamogeton coloratus	Fen Pondweed	P	floating	May–Sep	Shallow chalky water	
Potamogeton compressus	Grass-wrack Pondweed	P	floating	Jun–Sep	Lakes, ponds, ditches, streams	
Potamogeton crispus	Curled Pondweed	P	floating	May–Sep	Lakes, ponds, steams, canals	
Potamogeton epihydrus	American Pondweed	P	floating	Jun–Sep	Ponds, lakes	
Potamogeton filiformis	Slender-leaved Pondweed	P	floating	Jun–Sep	Brackish water, lakes near coast	
Potamogeton friesii	Flat-stalked Pondweed	P	floating	Jun–Sep	Ponds, lakes, ditches, canals	
Potamogeton gramineus	Various-leaved Pondweed	P	floating	Jun–Aug	Acid waters	
Potamogeton lucens	Shining Pondweed	P	floating	Jun–Sep	Deep chalky water	
Potamogeton natans	Broad-leaved Pondweed	P	floating	May–Sep	Rich organic, lakes, ditches, ponds	
Potamogeton nodosus	Loddon Pondweed	P	floating	May–Sep	Chalky waters, lakes, ditches, ponds	
Potamogeton obtusifolius	Blunt-leaved Pondweed	P	floating	Jun–Sep	Lakes, ponds, streams, ditches	
Potamogeton pectinatus	Fennel Pondweed	P	floating	Jun–Sep	Chalky, brackish, ponds, ditches	
Potamogeton perfoliatus	Perfoliate Pondweed	P	floating	Jun–Sep	Lakes, ponds, canals, ditches	
Potamogeton polygonifolius	Bog Pondweed	P	floating	May–Sep	Very shallow acid waters	
Potamogeton praelongus	Long-stalked Pondweed	P	floating	Jun–Sep	Lakes, ponds, ditches	
Potamogeton pusillus	Lesser Pondweed	P	floating	Jun–Sep	Chalky, brackish, ponds, ditches, lakes	
Potamogeton rutilus	Shetland Pondweed	P	floating	Jun–Sep	Ponds, lakes	
Potamogeton trichoides	Hairlike Pondweed	P	floating	Jun–Sep	Ponds, lakes, canals, ditches	
Potentilla anglica	Trailing Tormentil	P	up to 10 cm	Jun–Sep	Grassy, woods, banks, road verges	
Potentilla anserina	Silverweed	P	up to 30 cm	May–Aug	All soils	
Potentilla argentea	Hoary Cinquefoil	P	up to 60 cm	Jun–Sep	All soils	
Potentilla crantzii	Alpine Cinquefoil	P	up to 30 cm	Jun–Jul	Chalky, grassy, rocky, ledges	
Potentilla erecta	Tormentil	P	up to 10 cm	May–Sep	Grassy, all soils	
Potentilla fruticosa	Shrubby Cinquefoil	P	up to 1 m	May–Jul	Damp, chalky, rocky	
Potentilla neumanniana	Spring Cinquefoil	P	up to 30 cm	Apr–Jun	Dry, chalky, rocky, grassy	
Potentilla palustris	Marsh Cinquefoil	P	up to 60 cm	May–Jul	Wet, marshes, meadows, fens	
Potentilla reptans	Creeping Cinquefoil	P	up to 10 cm	Jun–Sep	Chalky, waste, banks, cultivated land	
Potentilla rupestris	Rock Cinquefoil	P	up to 60 cm	May–Jun	Rocky, ledges, woods	
Potentilla sterilis	Barren Strawberry	P	up to 10 cm	Feb–May	Dry, chalky, grassy, scrub, walls, road verges	
Primula elatior	Oxlip	P	up to 30 cm	Apr–May	Damp, grassy, woods, stream banks	
Primula farinosa	Bird's-eye Primrose	P	up to 10 cm	May–Aug	Damp, grassy, peaty	86
Primula scotica	Scottish Primrose	P	up to 10 cm	May–Jun	Coastal, grassy, heaths, dunes	
Primula veris	Cowslip	P	up to 30 cm	Apr–May	Dry, chalky, grassy, woods, banks	27
Primula vulgaris	Primrose	P	up to 10 cm	Dec–May	Damp, shady, grassy, banks, woods	
Prunella vulgaris	Selfheal	P	up to 30 cm	Jun–Nov	Dry, chalky, grassy, meadows, roadsides	
Prunus avium	Wild Cherry	T	up to 25 m	Apr–May	Well-drained, woods, hedgerows	
Prunus padus	Bird Cherry	T	up to 17 m	May–Jun	Woods, moors, scrub, hedgerows	
Prunus spinosa	Blackthorn	T	up to 1.4 m	Mar–May	Woods, scrub, hedgerows	
Pseudorchis albida	Small-white Orchid	O	up to 30 cm	May–Jun	Grassy, meadows, hills, mountains	
Pteridium aquilinum	Bracken	P	up to 4 m	Apr–Oct	Dry, hills, heaths, moors	
Puccinellia distans	Reflexed Saltmarsh-grass	P	up to 65 cm	Jun–Sep	Coastal, dry salt marshes, rocky	
Puccinellia fasciculata	Borrer's Saltmarsh-grass	P	up to 85 cm	Jun–Sep	Coastal, dry, muddy	
Puccinellia maritima	Common Saltmarsh-grass	P	up to 30 cm	Jun–Jul	Salt marshes	
Puccinellia rupestris	Stiff Saltmarsh-grass	A/Bi	up to 40 cm	May–Aug	Coastal, bare ground	
Pulicaria dysenterica	Common Fleabane	P	up to 60 cm	Aug–Sep	Damp, marshes, meadows, riverbanks	
Pulicaria vulgaris	Small Fleabane	A	up to 30 cm	Aug–Sep	Wet, sandy, river and stream banks	
Pulmonaria longifolia	Narrow-leaved Lungwort	P	up to 60 cm	Apr–Jun	Heavy clay, shady, rocky	
Pulmonaria obscura	Unspotted Lungwort	P	up to 30 cm	Mar–May	Shady, limestone, humus-rich soils	
Pulsatilla vulgaris	Pasqueflower	P	up to 10 cm	Apr–Jun	Limestone, grassy, meadows	86
Pyrola media	Intermediate Wintergreen	P	up to 60 cm	Jun–Aug	Humus-rich, pine woods, heaths, moors	
Pyrola minor	Common Wintergreen	P	up to 30 cm	Jun–Aug	Damp, chalky, rocky, moors, woods, mountains	
Pyrola rotundifolia	Round-leaved Wintergreen	P	up to 30 cm	Jun–Sep	Woods, rocky, bogs, fens	
Pyrus cordata	Plymouth Pear	T	up to 8 m	Apr–May	Scrub, woods, hedges	
Quercus petraea	Sessile Oak	T	up to 40 m	Apr–May	Poor soils, woods, hedgerows	
Quercus robur	Pedunculate Oak	T	up to 45 m	Apr–May	All soils, woods, hedgerows	
Radiola linoides	Allseed	A	up to 8 cm	Jul–Aug	All soils, grassy	
Ranunculus acris	Meadow Buttercup	P	up to 90 cm	Apr–Sep	Damp, grassy, meadows, road verges	
Ranunculus aquatilis	Common Water-crowfoot	P	floating	Apr–Sep	Freshwater, shallow, ponds, streams	

BOTANICAL NAME	COMMON NAME	TYPE	MAX. HEIGHT	FLOWERS	HABITATS	PAGE
Ranunculus arvensis	Corn Buttercup	A	up to 60 cm	May–Jul	Chalky, clay, arable, waste	
Ranunculus auricomus	Goldilocks Buttercup	P	up to 30 cm	Apr–May	Woods, meadows, rocky	
Ranunculus baudotii	Brackish Water-crowfoot	A/P	floating	May–Sep	Coastal, brackish water, ditches, pools, dykes	
Ranunculus bulbosus	Bulbous Buttercup	P	up to 60 cm	Mar–Jul	Chalky, acid, grassy	
Ranunculus circinatus	Fan-leaved Water-crowfoot	P	submerged	Jun–Aug	Freshwater, lakes, ponds, ditches	
Ranunculus ficaria	Lesser Celandine	P	up to 30 cm	Mar–May	All soils	
Ranunculus flammula	Lesser Spearwort	P	up to 60 cm	May–Sep	Wet, chalky, meadows, marshes, fens, pools	
Ranunculus fluitans	River Water-crowfoot	P	up to 1 m	Jun–Aug	Fast-flowing water over rocks	
Ranunculus hederaceus	Ivy-leaved Crowfoot	A/Bi	up to 40 cm	May–Sep	Shallow muddy freshwater	
Ranunculus lingua	Greater Spearwort	P	up to 90 cm	Jun–Sep	Shallow freshwater	37
Ranunculus omiophyllus	Round-leaved Crowfoot	A/Bi	up to 30 cm	Jun–Aug	Muddy freshwater	
Ranunculus ophioglossifolius	Adder's-tongue Spearwort	A	up to 30 cm	May–Aug	Freshwater marshes	
Ranunculus paludosus	Jersey Buttercup	P	up to 60 cm	May–Jun	Dry ground	
Ranunculus parviflorus	Small-flowered Buttercup	A	up to 30 cm	May–Jul	Dry, grassy, road verges, banks	
Ranunculus peltatus	Pond Water-crowfoot	A/P	floating	May–Aug	Shallow freshwater, lakes, ponds, ditches	
Ranunculus penicillatus	Stream Water-crowfoot	P	up to 5 m	Jun–Jul	Limestone, fast flowing river and streams	
Ranunculus repens	Creeping Buttercup	P	up to 60 cm	May–Sep	Grassy, chalky, marshes, fens, roadsides	
Ranunculus reptans	Creeping Spearwort	P	up to 60 cm	Jun–Aug	Gravel, lakesides	
Ranunculus sardous	Hairy Buttercup	A	up to 60 cm	May–Oct	Damp, grassy, arable, waste	
Ranunculus sceleratus	Celery-leaved Buttercup	A	up to 60 cm	May–Sep	Wet, marshes, meadows, stream and river margins	
Ranunculus trichophyllus	Thread-leaved Water-crowfoot	A/P	floating	May–Jul	Freshwater, shallow, streams, pools, ditches	
Ranunculus tripartitus	Three-lobed Crowfoot	A/P	floating	Mar–Jul	Shallow muddy freshwater, ditches, pools	87
Raphanus raphanistrum	Sea Radish	A/Bi	up to 90 cm	May–Sep	Clay, cultivated land, waste	
Reseda lutea	Wild Mignonette	P/Bi	up to 90 cm	Jun–Sep	Chalky, waste, cult. land, roadsides	87
Reseda luteola	Weld	Bi	up to 1.5 m	Jun–Sep	Chalky, stony, sandy, waste, quarries	88
Rhamnus cathartica	Buckthorn	T	up to 6 m	May–Jun	Chalky, scrub, woods, hedgerows	
Rhinanthus angustifolius	Greater Yellow-rattle	A	up to 60 cm	Jun–Sep	Grassy, meadows	
Rhinanthus minor	Yellow-rattle	A	up to 60 cm	May–Sep	Chalky, grassy, meadows, fens	27, 88
Rhynchospora alba	White Beak-sedge	P	up to 40 cm	Jun–Sep	Acid, peaty, moors, heaths	
Rhynchospora fusca	Brown Beak-sedge	P	up to 30 cm	May–Jul	Wet, acid, peaty, heaths, bogs	
Ribes alpinum	Mountain Currant	P	up to 2 m	Apr–May	Limestone, rocky, cliffs, woods	
Ribes nigrum	Black Currant	P	up to 2 m	Apr–May	Wet, hedgerows, woods, stream banks	88
Ribes spicatum	Downy Currant	P	up to 1.5 m	Apr–May	Chalky, rocky, woods	
Ribes uva-crispa	Gooseberry	P	up to 1.5 m	Mar–May	Waste, woods, hedgerows, scrub	
Romulea columnae	Sand Crocus	P	up to 10 cm	Apr–May	Coastal, sandy, grassy	
Rorippa amphibia	Great Yellow-cress	P	up to 90 cm	Jun–Aug	Wet, fertile soils, ponds, ditches, streams	
Rorippa islandica	Northern Yellow-cress	A/Bi	up to 60 cm	Jun–Aug	Damp, bare ground, stream and lake edges	
Rorippa microphylla	Narrow-fruited Water-cress	P	up to 60 cm	May–Oct	Shallow freshwater, streams, rivers, ditches	
Rorippa nasturtium-aquaticum	Water-cress	P	up to 60 cm	May–Oct	Shallow freshwater, streams, rivers, ditches	
Rorippa palustris	Marsh Yellow-cress	P	up to 60 cm	Jun–Aug	Damp, bare ground, stream and lake edges	
Rorippa sylvestris	Creeping Yellow-cress	P	up to 60 cm	Jun–Sep	Damp, bare ground, stream and pond edges	
Rosa agrestis	Small-leaved Sweet-briar	P	up to 2 m	Jun–Jul	Chalky, scrub, woods, hedgerows, banks	
Rosa arvensis	Field-rose	P	up to 3 m	Jun–Aug	Heavy soils, scrub, woods, hedges	90
Rosa caesia	Hairy Dog-rose	P	up to 3 m	Jun–Aug	Hedges, scrub, mainly N. England	
Rosa canina	Dog-rose	P	up to 5 m	Jun–Aug	Grassy, hedgerows, road verges, woods	91
Rosa micrantha	Small-flowered Sweet-briar	P	up to 2 m	Jun–Jul	Chalky, pastures, heaths	
Rosa mollis	Soft Downy-rose	P	up to 1.5 m	Jun–Jul	Chalky, scrub, woods, hedgerows	
Rosa obtusifolia	Round-leaved Dog-rose	P	up to 2 m	Jun–Aug	Grassy, scrub, banks	
Rosa pimpinellifolia	Burnet Rose	P	up to 1 m	May–Jul	Dry, chalky, limestone, heaths, sand dunes	90
Rosa rubiginosa	Sweet-briar	P	up to 3 m	Jun–Jul	Grassy, scrub, banks, coastal shingle	91
Rosa sherardii	Sherard's Downy-rose	P	up to 3 m	Jun–Jul	Woods, scrub, hedgerows	
Rosa stylosa	Short-styled Field-rose	P	up to 3 m	Jun–Jul	Grassy, woods, hedges	
Rosa tomentosa	Harsh Downy-rose	P	up to 2 m	Jun–Jul	Scrub, hedges, railway banks, hills	
Rubia peregrina	Wild Madder	P	up to 90 cm	Jun–Aug	Woods, scrub	
Rubus caesius	Dewberry	P	up to 60 cm	May–Sep	Damp, limestone, grassy, scrub	
Rubus chamaemorus	Cloudberry	P	up to 30 cm	Jun–Aug	Damp, acid, peaty, moors, bogs	
Rubus fruticosus	Bramble Raspberry	P	up to 3 m	May–Sep	All soils	92
Rubus saxatilis	Stone Bramble	P	up to 60 cm	Jun–Aug	Damp, shady, chalky, woods, screes	
Rumex acetosa	Common Sorrel	P	up to 90 cm	May–Jun	Woods, verges, meadows, coastal shingle	92
Rumex acetosella	Sheep's Sorrel	P	up to 30 cm	May–Aug	Dry, sandy, grassy, meadows, heaths, coastal	
Rumex aquaticus	Scottish Dock	P	up to 2 m	Jul–Aug	Wet, marshes, swamps	
Rumex conglomeratus	Clustered Dock	P	up to 90 cm	Jun–Oct	Damp, grassy, meadows, ditches, stream and pond edges	
Rumex crispus	Curled Dock	P	up to 90 cm	Jun–Oct	Damp, all soils	
Rumex hydrolapathum	Water Dock	P	up to 2 m	Jul–Sep	Shallow water, marshes, rivers, streams, ditches	
Rumex longifolius	Northern Dock	P	up to 90 cm	Jun–Jul	Damp, grassy, meadows, river and lake margins	
Rumex maritimus	Golden Dock	A	up to 60 cm	Jun–Sep	Coastal seashores, river and pond margins, ditches	
Rumex obtusifolius	Broad-leaved Dock	P	up to 1 m	Jun–Oct	Waste, meadows, hedgerows, pond and lake edges	
Rumex palustris	Marsh Dock	A/Bi	up to 60 cm	Jun–Sep	Muddy, marshes, gravel pits, pond and river edges	

BOTANICAL NAME	COMMON NAME	TYPE	MAX. HEIGHT	FLOWERS	HABITATS	PAGE
Rumex pulcher	Fiddle Dock	P	up to 60 cm	Jun–Aug	Dry, grassy, sandy, chalky, waste, roadsides	
Rumex rupestris	Shore Dock	P	up to 1.2 cm	Jun–Aug	Coastal habitats	
Rumex sanguineus	Blood-veined Dock	P	up to 100 cm	Jun–Aug	Damp, shady, heavy soils, waste, woods, verges	
Ruppia cirrhosa	Spiral Tasselweed	P	floating	Jul–Sep	Aquatic submerged, coastal, brackish water	
Ruppia maritima	Beaked Tasselweed	P	up to 30 cm	Jul–Sep	Aquatic submerged, coastal, brackish water	
Ruscus aculeatus	Butcher's-broom	P	up to 90 cm	Jan–Apr	Chalky, woods, hedges, sea cliffs	
Sagina apetala	Annual Pearlwort	A	up to 10 cm	Apr–Aug	Dry, grassy, sandy, walls	
Sagina boydii	Boyd's Pearlwort	P	up to 2 cm	Jul–Sep	Very rare, origin enigmatic, probably Scotland	
Sagina maritima	Sea Pearlwort	A	up to 10 cm	May–Sep	Coastal	
Sagina nivalis	Snow Pearlwort	P	up to 10 cm	Jun–Sep	Rocky, screes	
Sagina nodosa	Knotted Pearlwort	P	up to 10 cm	Jul–Sep	Damp, grassy	
Sagina procumbens	Procumbent Pearlwort	P	up to 10 cm	May–Sep	Damp, shady, walls	
Sagina saginoides	Alpine Pearlwort	P	up to 10 cm	Jun–Sep	Damp, rocky, mountains	
Sagina subulata	Heath Pearlwort	P	up to 10 cm	May–Aug	Dry, sandy, gravelly, heaths	
Sagittaria sagittifolia	Arrowhead	P	up to 90 cm	Jul–Aug	Aquatic freshwater	
Salicornia dolichostachya	Long-spiked Glasswort	A	up to 45 cm	Jul–Aug	Muddy, sandy, coastal estuaries	
Salicornia europaea	Common Glasswort	A	up to 60 cm	Aug–Sep	Coastal, muddy, salt marshes	
Salicornia fragilis	Yellow Glasswort	A	up to 40 cm	Aug–Sep	Sandy, bare, muddy, salt marshes	
Salicornia nitens	Shiny Glasswort	A	up to 30 cm	Aug–Sep	Coastal, muddy, salt marshes	
Salicornia obscura	Glaucous Glasswort	A	up to 40 cm	Aug–Sep	Bare mud in salt pans	
Salicornia pusilla	One-flowered Glasswort	A	up to 25 cm	Aug–Sep	Salt marshes, estuaries, sea walls	
Salicornia ramosissima	Purple Glasswort	A	up to 40 cm	Aug–Sep	Coastal, salt marshes, estuaries	
Salix alba	White Willow	T	up to 25 m	Apr–May	Damp, all soils	
Salix arbuscula	Mountain Willow	P	up to 1 m	May–Jun	Damp, mountain, slopes, ledges	
Salix aurita	Eared Willow	P	up to 2 m	Apr–Jun	Damp, heaths, moors, woods, stream and lake edges	
Salix caprea	Goat Willow	T	up to 10 m	Mar–Apr	Damp, scrub, hedges, woods	
Salix cinerea	Grey Willow	P	up to 6 m	Mar–Apr	Damp, marshes, fens, woods, stream and lake edges	
Salix fragilis	Crack-willow	T	up to 25 m	Apr–May	Freshwater margins, damp woods	
Salix herbacea	Dwarf Willow	P	up to 100 cm	Jun–Jul	Rocky, ledges, mountains	
Salix lanata	Woolly Willow	P	up to 3 m	May–Jul	Damp, rocky, ledges, mountains	
Salix lapponum	Downy Willow	P	up to 1.5 m	May–Jun	Wet, rocky, cliffs	
Salix myrsinifolia	Dark-leaved Willow	T	up to 4 m	Apr–May	Damp, rocky, ledges, lake and stream edges	
Salix myrsinites	Whortle-leaved Willow	P	up to 40 cm	May–Jun	Wet, rocky	
Salix pentandra	Bay Willow	T	up to 7 m	May–Jun	Damp habitats	
Salix phylicifolia	Tea-leaved Willow	P	up to 4 m	Apr–May	Wet, rocky, stony, stream and lake margins	
Salix purpurea	Purple Willow	P	up to 5 m	Mar–Apr	Marshes, fens, lake and pond edges	
Salix repens	Creeping Willow	P	up to 1.5 m	Apr–May	Wet, bogs, fens, heaths	
Salix reticulata	Net-leaved Willow	P	up to 100 cm	Jun–Aug	Rocky, ledges, mountains	
Salix triandra	Almond Willow	T	up to 10 m	Apr–May	Marshes, fens, ponds and river banks	
Salix viminalis	Osier	T	up to 5 m	Mar–Apr	Marshes, fens, lakes, streams	
Salsola kali	Prickly Saltwort	A	up to 60 cm	Jul–Oct	Coastal, sandy	
Salvia pratensis	Meadow Clary	P	up to 90 cm	Jun–Jul	Grassy, chalky, meadows, waste	15
Salvia verbenaca	Wild Clary	P	up to 90 cm	May–Aug	Dry, grassy, chalky, sandy, roadsides	
Sambucus ebulus	Dwarf Elder	P	up to 2 m	Jul–Aug	Road verges, hedges	
Sambucus nigra	Elder	T	up to 10 m	Jun–Jul	Chalky, nitrogen-rich, woods, waste, hedges	
Samolus valerandi	Brookweed	P	up to 30 cm	Jun–Aug	Chalky, damp, shady, rocky, coastal sandy	
Sanguisorba minor	Salad Burnet	P	up to 30 cm	May–Sep	Dry, chalky, limestone, grassy, rocky	
Sanguisorba officinalis	Great Burnet	P	up to 90 cm	Jun–Sep	Damp meadows	
Sanicula europaea	Sanicle	P	up to 60 cm	May–Aug	Chalky, deciduous woods (oak, ash, beech)	
Saponaria officinalis	Soapwort	P	up to 90 cm	Jun–Sep	Woods, hedges, waste, road verges	
Sarcocornia perennis	Perennial Glasswort	P	up to 1 m	Aug–Oct	Coastal, gravelly, salt marshes	
Saussurea alpina	Alpine Saw-wort	P	up to 60 cm	Jul–Sep	Chalky, grassy, rocky, mountains, cliffs, screes	
Saxifraga aizoides	Yellow Saxifrage	P	up to 30 cm	Jun–Sep	Damp, rocky, stream banks	
Saxifraga cernua	Drooping Saxifrage	P	up to 30 cm	Jun–Jul	Rocky, shady, ledges, mountains	
Saxifraga cespitosa	Tufted Saxifrage	P	up to 10 cm	May–Jul	Rocky, cliffs, mountains	
Saxifraga granulata	Meadow Saxifrage	P	up to 60 cm	Apr–Jun	Chalky, grassy, meadows, banks, roadsides	
Saxifraga hirculus	Marsh Saxifrage	P	up to 30 cm	Jun–Sep	Wet, grassy, bogs, moors, mountains	
Saxifraga hirsuta	Kidney Saxifrage	P	up to 30 cm	May–Jul	Damp, shady, rocky, mountains, stream banks	
Saxifraga hypnoides	Mossy Saxifrage	P	up to 30 cm	May–Jul	Damp, chalky, grassy, mountains, cliffs, screes	
Saxifraga nivalis	Alpine Saxifrage	P	up to 10 cm	Jul–Aug	Shady, rocky, mountains, ledges, screes	
Saxifraga oppositifolia	Purple Saxifrage	P	up to 10 cm	Mar–Aug	Damp, rocky, limestone, cliffs, mountains, screes	
Saxifraga rivularis	Highland Saxifrage	P	up to 10 cm	Jul–Aug	Wet, rocky, mountains	
Saxifraga rosacea	Irish Saxifrage	P	up to 30 cm	Jun–Aug	Cliffs, mountains, screes	
Saxifraga spathularis	St Patrick's-cabbage	P	up to 30 cm	Jun–Aug	Damp, acid, rocky, woods, stream margins	
Saxifraga stellaris	Starry Saxifrage	P	up to 30 cm	Jun–Aug	Damp, meadows, rocky, marshes, stream banks	
Saxifraga tridactylites	Rue-leaved Saxifrage	A	up to 30 cm	Jun–Sep	Grassy, rocky, limestone, dunes, heaths	
Scabiosa columbaria	Small Scabious	P	up to 60 cm	Jul–Aug	Dry, chalky, grassy	93
Scandix pecten-veneris	Shepherd's-needle	A	up to 30 cm	Apr–Aug	Waste, arable	

BOTANICAL NAME	COMMON NAME	TYPE	MAX. HEIGHT	FLOWERS	HABITATS	PAGE
Scheuchzeria palustris	Rannoch-rush	P	up to 30 cm	Jun–Aug	Aquatic, sphagnum bogs	
Schoenoplectus lacustris	Common Club-rush	P	up to 3 m	Jun–Aug	Rivers, streams, lakes	
Schoenoplectus pungens	Sharp Club-rush	P	up to 100 cm	Jun–Aug	Sandy, marshes, river banks	
Schoenoplectus tabernaemontani	Grey Club-rush	P	up to 1.7 m	Jun–Aug	Brackish water, rivers, streams, lakes	
Schoenoplectus triqueter	Triangular Club-rush	P	up to 1.5 m	Jun–Sep	Damp, muddy, rivers, estuaries	
Schoenus ferrugineus	Brown Bog-rush	P	up to 1.2 cm	Apr–Jul	Wet, peaty, acid soils	
Schoenus nigricans	Black Bog-rush	P	up to 1.2 cm	May–Jul	Peaty, fens, bogs	
Scilla autumnalis	Autumn Squill	P	up to 30 cm	Aug–Oct	Coastal, dry, rocky, grassy	
Scilla verna	Spring Squill	P	up to 30 cm	Apr–Jun	Grassy, rocky	19, 93
Scirpoides holoschoenus	Round-headed Club-rush	P	up to 1.5 m	Jun–Sep	Damp, coastal, sandy	
Scirpus sylvaticus	Wood Club-rush	P	up to 1.2 cm	May–Jul	Wet, shady, woods, fens, marshes	93
Scleranthus annuus	Annual Knawel	A/Bi	up to 10 cm	May–Oct	Dry, acid, grassy, sandy, gravelly	
Scleranthus perennis	Perennial Knawel	P	up to 30 cm	May–Oct	Dry, sandy, waste, cliffs	
Scorzonera humilis	Viper's-grass	P	up to 60 cm	May–Jul	Damp, acid, grassy, fields	
Scrophularia auriculata	Water Figwort	P	up to 1 m	Jun–Sep	Fens, marshes, river, stream and lake margins	
Scrophularia nodosa	Common Figwort	P	up to 90 cm	Jun–Sep	Damp, woods, hedgerows, river and stream margins	
Scrophularia scorodonia	Balm-leaved Figwort	P	up to 90 cm	Jun–Aug	Meadows, hedges, river and stream edges	
Scrophularia umbrosa	Green Figwort	P	up to 90 cm	Jun–Sep	Damp, shady, woods, banks, marshes, fens	
Scutellaria galericulata	Skullcap	P	up to 60 cm	Jun–Sep	Wet, grassy, chalky, water, margins	
Scutellaria minor	Lesser Skullcap	P	up to 30 cm	Jul–Oct	Damp, peaty, paths, rides	
Sedum acre	Biting Stonecrop	P	up to 10 cm	May–Jul	Sandy, rocky, shingle, banks, heaths, walls	
Sedum album	White Stonecrop	P	up to 30 cm	Jun–Aug	Rocky, screes, ledges, walls	
Sedum anglicum	English Stonecrop	P	up to 10 cm	Jun–Sep	Dry, grassy, rocky, acid, sandy, shingle	
Sedum forsterianum	Rock Stonecrop	P	up to 30 cm	Jun–Jul	Rocky, woods, screes, walls	
Sedum rosea	Roseroot	P	up to 30 cm	May–Jun	Chalky, acid, coastal, rocky, cliffs, screes	
Sedum telephium	Orpine	P	up to 90 cm	Jul–Sep	Shady, sandy, scrub, woods, hedges	94
Sedum villosum	Hairy Stonecrop	P/Bi	up to 10 cm	Jun–Aug	Wet, chalky, stony, pastures, stream and river banks	
Selaginella selaginoides	Lesser Clubmoss	P	up to 20 cm	Jul–Sep	Damp, grassy, dune slacks	
Selinum carvifolia	Cambridge Milk-parsley	P	up to 90 cm	Jul–Oct	Damp, fens, meadows	
Senecio aquaticus	Marsh Ragwort	Bi	up to 90 cm	Jul–Aug	Wet, marshes, meadows, stream and river edges	
Senecio cambrensis	Welsh Groundsel	A	up to 50 cm	May–Oct	Road verges, cultivated ground	
Senecio erucifolius	Hoary Ragwort	P	up to 90 cm	Jul–Sep	Chalky, clay, grassy, hedges, roadsides, coastal shingle	
Senecio jacobaea	Common Ragwort	P/Bi	up to 90 cm	Jun–Nov	All soils	94
Senecio paludosus	Fen Ragwort	P	up to 90 cm	May–Jul	Damp habitats, fens	
Senecio sylvaticus	Heath Groundsel	A	up to 60 cm	Jul–Sep	Acid, sandy, woods, heaths, waste, banks	
Senecio viscosus	Sticky Groundsel	A	up to 60 cm	Jul–Oct	Waste, road verges, coastal sand and gravel	
Senecio vulgaris	Groundsel	A	up to 30 cm	Jan–Dec	All soils, coastal	
Seriphidium maritimum	Sea Wormwood	P	up to 60 cm	Aug–Oct	Coastal, sandy, walls	
Serratula tinctoria	Saw-wort	P	up to 90 cm	Jul–Sep	Rough grassy, heaths, scrub, woods	
Seseli libanotis	Moon Carrot	P/Bi	up to 90 cm	Jul–Sep	Dry, chalky, grassy, scrub	94
Sesleria caerulea	Blue Moor-grass	P	up to 45 cm	Apr–Jun	Wet, acid, heaths, moors	
Sherardia arvensis	Field Madder	A	up to 10 cm	May–Sep	Arable, cornfields	
Sibbaldia procumbens	Sibbaldia	P	up to 10 cm	Jul–Aug	Grassy, rocky, mountains	
Sibthorpia europaea	Cornish Moneywort	P	up to 40 cm	Jul–Oct	Damp, shady, banks	
Silaum silaus	Pepper-saxifrage	P	up to 90 cm	Jun–Aug	Grassy, clay, banks, meadows, verges	
Silene acaulis	Moss Campion	P	up to 10 cm	Jun–Aug	Damp, rocky, mountains, short turf	
Silene conica	Sand Catchfly	A	up to 30 cm	May–Aug	Coastal, sandy, chalky, waste	
Silene dioica	Red Campion	P/Bi	up to 90 cm	May–Nov	Chalky, woods, hedgerows	95
Silene gallica	Small-flowered Catchfly	A	up to 60 cm	Jun–Oct	Sandy, gravelly, waste, arable	
Silene latifolia	White Campion	A/P	up to 90 cm	May–Oct	Dry, chalky, waste, arable	95
Silene noctiflora	Night-flowering Catchfly	A	up to 60 cm	Jun–Aug	Dry, sandy, waste, arable	
Silene nutans	Nottingham Catchfly	P	up to 60 cm	May–Aug	Dry, chalky, rocky, shingle, grassy	
Silene otites	Spanish Catchfly	P/Bi	up to 60 cm	Jun–Sep	Dry, chalky, sandy, grassy, banks, heaths	
Silene uniflora	Sea Campion	P	up to 60 cm	Jun–Aug	Coastal, cliffs, rocky, shingle	
Silene vulgaris	Bladder Campion	P	up to 90 cm	Jun–Aug	Dry, chalky, grassy, waste	95
Simethis planifolia	Kerry Lily	P	up to 30 cm	May–Jun	Rocky, heaths, pine woods	
Sinapis arvensis	Charlock	A	up to 90 cm	Apr–Oct	Chalky, arable, waste, banks	
Sison amomum	Stone Parsley	Bi	up to 80 cm	Jul–Sep	Heavy soils, grassy, banks, waste, road verges	
Sisymbrium officinale	Hedge Mustard	A/Bi	up to 90 cm	May–Sep	Waste, hedges, banks	
Sisyrinchium bermudiana	Blue-eyed-grass	P	up to 60 cm	Jul–Aug	Damp, grassy, lakesides	
Sium latifolium	Greater Water-parsnip	P	up to 1.5 m	Jun–Sep	Semi-aquatic, shallow freshwater	
Solanum dulcamara	Bittersweet	P	up to 2 m	Jun–Sep	Damp, scrub, woods, stream sides	
Solanum nigrum	Black Nightshade	A	up to 60 cm	Jul–Oct	Waste, bare ground, cultivated	
Solidago virgaurea	Goldenrod	P	up to 90 cm	Jul–Sep	Dry, chalky, acid	
Sonchus arvensis	Perennial Sow-thistle	P	up to 90 cm	Jul–Oct	Waste, marshes, banks, cultivated land, coastal sand and shingle	
Sonchus asper	Prickly Sow-thistle	A	up to 90 cm	Jun–Aug	Waste, fields, cultivated land	
Sonchus oleraceus	Smooth Sow-thistle	A	up to 90 cm	Jun–Aug	Waste, cultivated land, roadsides	
Sonchus palustris	Marsh Sow-thistle	P	up to 2.5 m	Jul–Sep	Wet, peaty, freshwater, brackish	

BOTANICAL NAME	COMMON NAME	TYPE	MAX. HEIGHT	FLOWERS	HABITATS	PAGE
Sorbus aria	Common Whitebeam	T	up to 25 m	May–Jun	Chalky, woods, scrub, hedgerows	
Sorbus aucuparia	Rowan	T	up to 15 m	May–Jun	Light soils, woods, hedges, moors, mountains	
Sorbus domestica	Service-tree	T	up to 20 m	May	Rocky, woods, hedgerows	
Sorbus rupicola	Rock Whitebeam	P	up to 2 m	Jun–Jul	Limestone, mountains, uplands	
Sorbus torminalis	Wild Service-tree	T	up to 25 m	May–Jun	Clay, scrub, woods	
Sparganium angustifolium	Floating Bur-reed	P	up to 1 m	Jul–Sep	Peaty pools, lake and river margins	
Sparganium emersum	Unbranched Bur-reed	P	up to 60 cm	Jul–Aug	Freshwater margins	
Sparganium erectum	Branched Bur-reed	P	up to 1.5 m	Jul–Aug	Freshwater margins, marshes	
Sparganium natans	Least Bur-reed	P	up to 30 cm	Jun–Jul	Ponds, lakes, ditches	
Spartina anglica	Common Cord-grass	P	up to 1.3 m	Jul–Nov	Coastal mud	
Spartina maritima	Small Cord-grass	P	up to 70 cm	Jul–Sep	Salt marshes	
Spergula arvensis	Corn Spurrey	A	up to 60 cm	May–Sep	Sandy, acid, arable, roadsides, seashores	
Spergularia bocconei	Greek Sea-spurrey	A/Bi	up to 30 cm	May–Sep	Coastal, sandy, rocky, waste, gravel paths	
Spergularia marina	Lesser Sea-spurrey	A/Bi	up to 30 cm	May–Sep	Coastal seashores, salt marshes	
Spergularia media	Greater Sea-spurrey	P	up to 30 cm	May–Sep	Salt marshes, sandy, gravelly	
Spergularia rubra	Sand Spurrey	A/P	up to 30 cm	Jun–Sep	Dry, sandy, heaths, cliffs	
Spergularia rupicola	Rock Sea-spurrey	P	up to 30 cm	May–Sep	Coastal, rocky, cliffs, screes	
Spiranthes aestivalis	Summer Lady's-tresses	P	up to 35 cm	Jul–Aug	Wet habitats	
Spiranthes romanzoffiana	Irish Lady's-tresses	P	up to 30 cm	Aug–Sep	Damp, peaty	
Spiranthes spiralis	Autumn Lady's-tresses	O	up to 30 cm	Aug–Sep	Dry, grassy	96
Spirodela polyrhiza	Greater Duckweed	P	up to 5 mm	Jul	Freshwater, ponds, lakes, ditches	
Stachys alpina	Limestone Woundwort	P	up to 90 cm	Jun–Aug	Damp, rocky, limestone, woods	
Stachys arvensis	Field Woundwort	A	up to 30 cm	Apr–Nov	Acid, arable, sandy	
Stachys germanica	Downy Woundwort	P/Bi	up to 90 cm	Jul–Sep	Grassy, roadsides, ledges	
Stachys officinalis	Betony	P	up to 90 cm	Jun–Oct	Light soils, grassy, heaths, woods, banks	
Stachys palustris	Marsh Woundwort	P	up to 90 cm	Jun–Oct	Damp, arable, river, stream, pond margins	96
Stachys sylvatica	Hedge Woundwort	P	up to 1.2 m	Jun–Oct	Shady, banks, hedges, woods	96
Stellaria graminea	Lesser Stitchwort	P	up to 90 cm	May–Aug	Chalky, grassy, woods, hedge banks, heaths	
Stellaria holostea	Greater Stitchwort	P	up to 60 cm	Apr–Jun	Woods, hedges, roadsides, banks	
Stellaria media	Common Chickweed	A	up to 30 cm	Jan–Dec	Shingle, waste, roadsides, cultivated land	
Stellaria neglecta	Greater Chickweed	A	up to 60 cm	Apr–Jul	Damp, shady, ledges, woods, stream banks	
Stellaria nemorum	Wood Stitchwort	P	up to 60 cm	May–Jul	Damp, woods, stream banks	
Stellaria pallida	Lesser Chickweed	A	up to 30 cm	Mar–May	Arable, light sandy, grassy, banks, waste	
Stellaria palustris	Marsh Stitchwort	P	up to 60 cm	May–Jul	Chalky, grassy, marshes, fens	
Stellaria uliginosa	Bog Stitchwort	P	up to 30 cm	May–Jun	Damp, acid, marshes, bogs, stream banks	
Stratiotes aloides	Water-soldier	P	up to 40 cm	Jun–Aug	Aquatic, submerged	
Suaeda maritima	Annual Sea-blite	A	up to 60 cm	Jul–Sep	Coastal, salt marshes	
Suaeda vera	Shrubby Sea-blite	P	up to 1.2 m	Jun–Oct	Coastal, shingle, sandy, rocky, salt marshes	
Subularia aquatica	Awlwort	A	up to 10 cm	Jun–Sep	Aquatic	
Succisa pratensis	Devil's-bit Scabious	P	up to 90 cm	Jul–Oct	Shallow, gravelly, pools, lakes, mountains	
Symphytum officinale	Common Comfrey	P	up to 1.2 m	May–Jul	Damp, grassy, fens, ditches, river and stream banks	97
Symphytum tuberosum	Tuberous Comfrey	P	up to 60 cm	May–Jul	Damp, shady	
Tamus communis	Black Bryony	P	up to 4 m	May–Aug	Woods, hedges, scrub	97
Tanacetum parthenium	Feverfew	Bi/P	up to 60 cm	Jul–Sep	Chalky, rocky, scrub, banks, walls, cultivated land	
Tanacetum vulgare	Tansy	P	up to 1.5 m	Jul–Sep	All soils	
Taraxacum officinale	Dandelion	P	up to 40 cm	Mar–Oct	Grassy, cult. land	97
Taxus baccata	Yew	T	up to 20 m	Feb–Apr	Chalky, woods, scrub, hedges	
Teesdalia nudicaulis	Shepherd's Cress	A	up to 30 cm	May–Oct	Coastal, sandy, gravelly, acid heaths	
Tephroseris integrifolia	Field Fleawort	P	up to 60 cm	May–Jun	Dry, grassy, chalky, banks, hills	
Tephroseris palustris	Marsh Fleawort	A/P	up to 2 m	Jun–Jul	Damp, fens, marshes, meadows	
Teucrium botrys	Cut-leaved Germander	A/Bi	up to 30 cm	Jun–Oct	Dry, chalky, rocky, grassy	
Teucrium chamaedrys	Wall Germander	P	up to 30 cm	May–Sep	Dry, walls, ruins	
Teucrium scordium	Water Germander	P	up to 30 cm	Jun–Oct	Damp, chalky	
Teucrium scorodonia	Wood Sage	P	up to 60 cm	Jul–Sep	Dry, dunes, woods	
Thalictrum alpinum	Alpine Meadow-rue	P	up to 30 cm	May–Jul	Damp, chalky, rocky, ledges, grassy mountains	
Thalictrum flavum	Common Meadow-rue	P	up to 90 cm	Jun–Aug	Wet, chalky, grassy, marshes, fens, meadows	
Thalictrum minus	Lesser Meadow-rue	P	up to 80 cm	Jun–Aug	Chalky, damp, grassy, rocky, sand dunes, cliffs	
Thelypteris palustris	Marsh Fern	P	up to 1.5 m	Jun–Oct	Marshes, fens	
Thesium humifusum	Bastard-toadflax	P	up to 30 cm	Jun–Aug	Dry, chalky, grassy	
Thlaspi arvense	Field Penny-cress	A	up to 60 cm	May–Aug	Waste, arable	
Thlaspi caerulescens	Alpine Penny-cress	Bi	up to 60 cm	Apr–Jul	Limestone, rocky, screes, mountains woods	
Thlaspi perfoliatum	Perfoliate Penny-cress	A	up to 30 cm	May–Aug	Waste, arable, banks, walls	
Thymus polytrichus	Wild Garden	P	up to 10 cm	May–Sep	Grassy, meadows, pastures, paths	
Thymus pulegioides	Large Garden	P	up to 60 cm	Jun–Sep	Dry, chalky, grassy, banks	
Thymus serpyllum	Breckland Garden	P	up to 10 cm	May–Sep	Dry, grassy, heaths, scrub, sand dunes	
Tilia cordata	Small-leaved Lime	T	up to 30 m	Jun–Jul	Woods, limestone cliffs	
Tilia platyphyllos	Large-leaved Lime	T	up to 40 m	Jun–Jul	Chalky, woods	
Tofieldia pusilla	Scottish Asphodel	P	up to 30 cm	Jun–Aug	Wet, rocky, mountains, meadows	

BOTANICAL NAME	COMMON NAME	TYPE	MAX. HEIGHT	FLOWERS	HABITATS	PAGE
Torilis arvensis	Spreading Hedge-parsley	A	up to 30 cm	Jul–Sep	Dry, chalky, arable, cult. land	
Torilis japonica	Upright Hedge-parsley	A	up to 1.25 m	Jul–Sep	Dry, grassy	
Torilis nodosa	Knotted Hedge-parsley	A	up to 30 cm	May–Jul	Dry, grassy, bare ground	
Tragopogon pratensis	Goat's-beard	P/A	up to 90 cm	Jun–Jul	Rough grassy, waste	
Trichomanes speciosum	Killarney Fern	P	up to 35 cm	Jul–Sep	Rocks by freshwater	
Trichophorum alpinum	Cotton Deergrass	P	up to 35 cm	May–Jun	Base-rich peat	
Trichophorum cespitosum	Deergrass	P	up to 35 cm	May–Jun	Acid, heaths, moors, bogs	
Trientalis europaea	Chickweed-wintergreen	P	up to 30 cm	Jun–Jul	Damp, acid, grassy, mossy, conif. woods	98
Trifolium arvense	Hare's-foot Clover	A/Bi	up to 30 cm	Jun–Sep	Dry, grassy, road verges, waste	
Trifolium bocconei	Twin-headed Clover	A/Bi	up to 30 cm	May–Jun	Coastal, dry, grassy	
Trifolium campestre	Hop Trefoil	A	up to 30 cm	Jun–Sep	Dry, grassy, road verges, sand dunes	
Trifolium dubium	Lesser Trefoil	A	up to 30 cm	May–Oct	Dry, grassy, road verges, lawns, commons	
Trifolium fragiferum	Strawberry Clover	P	up to 10 cm	Jul–Sep	Short grassy, heavy clay, pastures, commons	
Trifolium glomeratum	Clustered Clover	A	up to 20 cm	Jun–Aug	Dry, grassy, walls, coastal sand and gravel	
Trifolium incarnatum	Long-headed Clover	A	up to 60 cm	May–Sep	Waste, fields, forage crop	
Trifolium medium	Zigzag Clover	P	up to 60 cm	May–Jul	Grassy, scrub, woods	
Trifolium micranthum	Slender Trefoil	A	up to 10 cm	Jun–Aug	Dry, grassy, sandy, gravelly, waste	
Trifolium occidentale	Western Clover	P	up to 30 cm	Apr–Jul	Coastal, rocky, sandy, grassy	
Trifolium ochroleucon	Sulphur Clover	P	up to 60 cm	Jun–Jul	Damp, shady, clay soils, grassy	
Trifolium ornithopodioides	Bird's-foot Clover	A	up to 10 cm	May–Sep	Dry, sandy, gravelly, coastal cliffs	
Trifolium pratense	Red Clover	P	up to 90 cm	May–Sep	Damp, chalky, grassy, cult. land	
Trifolium repens	White Clover	P	up to 30 cm	Jun–Sep	All soils	
Trifolium scabrum	Rough Clover	A	up to 30 cm	May–Jul	All soils	
Trifolium squamosum	Sea Clover	A	up to 60 cm	Jun–Jul	Coastal, grassy, salt marshes, estuaries	
Trifolium striatum	Knotted Clover	A/Bi	up to 30 cm	May–Jul	Grassy, banks, heaths, dunes	
Trifolium strictum	Upright Clover	A	up to 30 cm	May–Jul	Acid, short grassy	
Trifolium subterraneum	Subterranean Clover	A	up to 10 cm	May–Jun	Dry, grassy, coastal, sandy, gravelly, cliffs	
Trifolium suffocatum	Suffocated Clover	A	up to 10 cm	Mar–May	Dry, coastal, sand dunes, grassy	
Triglochin maritimum	Sea Arrowgrass	P	up to 60 cm	May–Sep	Coastal, marshes, short turf	
Triglochin palustre	Marsh Arrowgrass	P	up to 90 cm	May–Aug	Marshes, fens, meadows, stream sides	
Trinia glauca	Honewort	P	up to 30 cm	May–Jun	Limestone, dry, grassy	
Tripleurospermum inodorum	Scentless Mayweed	P/Bi	up to 60 cm	Jul–Sep	All soils	
Tripleurospermum maritimum	Sea Mayweed	P/Bi	up to 60 cm	Jul–Sep	Coastal habitats	
Trisetum flavescens	Yellow Oat-grass	P	up to 80 cm	Jun–Jul	Chalky, grassy	
Trollius europaeus	Globeflower	P	up to 60 cm	May–Aug	Damp, woods, fens, meadows	
Tuberaria guttata	Spotted Rock-rose	A	up to 30 cm	May–Aug	Acid, rocky, sea cliffs	
Tussilago farfara	Colt's-foot	P	up to 30 cm	Feb–Apr	Damp, chalky, clay, arable, banks, roadsides	
Typha angustifolia	Lesser Bulrush	P	up to 2 m	Jul–Aug	Freshwater margins	
Typha latifolia	Bulrush	P	up to 2 m	Jul–Aug	Freshwater, lakes, marshes, ponds	
Ulex europaeus	Gorse	P	up to 2 m	Jan–Dec	Grassy, heaths, scrub, road verges, banks	
Ulex gallii	Western Gorse	P	up to 60 cm	Jul–Nov	Acid, grassy, heaths, banks	
Ulex minor	Dwarf Gorse	P	up to 100 cm	Jul–Nov	Grassy, banks, heaths, road verges	
Ulmus glabra	Wych Elm	T	up to 40 m	Mar–Apr	Woods, hedgerows	
Ulmus minor	Small-leaved Elm	T	up to 30 m	Mar–Apr	Woods, hedges, fields	
Ulmus plotii	Plot's Elm	T	up to 30 m	Mar–Apr	Woods, hedges	
Ulmus procera	English Elm	T	up to 30 m	Mar–Apr	Fields, hedgerows	
Umbilicus rupestris	Navelwort	P	up to 60 cm	Jun–Aug	Acid, rocky, grassy, banks, walls, cliffs, mountains	98
Urtica dioica	Common Nettle	P	up to 90 cm	Jun–Sep	All soils	99
Urtica urens	Small Nettle	A	up to 60 cm	Jun–Oct	Waste, gardens	
Utricularia australis	Bladderwort	P	up to 45 cm	Jul–Aug	Floating and submerged aquatic, acid waters	
Utricularia intermedia	Intermediate Bladderwort	P	up to 25 cm	Jul–Sep	Shallow ponds, lakes, ditches, acid peaty waters	
Utricularia minor	Lesser Bladderwort	P	up to 25 cm	Jun–Sep	Shallow peaty water, bogs, ponds	
Utricularia ochroleuca	Pale Bladderwort	P	up to 25 cm	Jul–Sep	Still, shallow water, peat bogs	
Utricularia stygia	Nordic Bladderwort	P	up to 20 cm	Jul–Sep	Shallow water, peat bogs	
Utricularia vulgaris	Greater Bladderwort	P	up to 45 cm	Jul–Aug	Floating and submerged aquatic	
Vaccinium microcarpum	Small Cranberry	P	up to 10 cm	Jul–Aug	Peat, bogs	
Vaccinium myrtillus	Bilberry	P	up to 60 cm	Apr–Jun	Dry, acid, heaths, woods, moors	
Vaccinium oxycoccos	Cranberry	P	up to 80 cm	Jun–Aug	Wet, acid, sphagnum bogs, heaths, woods	
Vaccinium uliginosum	Bog Bilberry	P	up to 75 cm	May–Jun	Damp, acid, heaths, woods, moors	
Vaccinium vitis-idaea	Cowberry	P	up to 20 cm	Jun–Aug	Moors, heaths, coniferous woods	
Valeriana dioica	Marsh Valerian	P	up to 60 cm	May–Jul	Wet, chalky, slightly acid	
Valeriana officinalis	Common Valerian	P	up to 1.5 m	Jun–Aug	Dry, chalky, scrub, meadows, woods	
Valerianella carinata	Keeled-fruited Cornsalad	A	up to 60 cm	Apr–Jun	Walls, rocky, arable	
Valerianella dentata	Narrow-fruited Cornsalad	A	up to 30 cm	Jun–Jul	Light soils, arable	
Valerianella locusta	Common Cornsalad	A	up to 60 cm	Apr–Jun	Chalky, sandy, arable, waste, cliffs	
Valerianella rimosa	Broad-fruited Cornsalad	A	up to 30 cm	Jul–Aug	Arable	
Verbascum lychnitis	White Mullein	Bi	up to 1.5 m	Jul–Aug	Chalky, rocky, waste, banks	
Verbascum nigrum	Dark Mullein	P	up to 90 cm	Jul–Oct	Dry, chalky, rocky, grassy, banks, roadsides	18, 100

Complete List

BOTANICAL NAME	COMMON NAME	TYPE	MAX. HEIGHT	FLOWERS	HABITATS	PAGE
Verbascum pulverulentum	Hoary Mullein	Bi	up to 90 cm	Jul–Aug	Rough grassy, waste, banks, roadsides	
Verbascum thapsus	Great Mullein	Bi	up to 2 m	Jun–Aug	Dry, gravelly, chalky, scrub, waste, banks	
Verbascum virgatum	Twiggy Mullein	Bi	up to 90 cm	Jun–Oct	Waste, cultivated land	
Verbena officinalis	Vervain	P	up to 60 cm	Jun–Oct	Rough grassy, rocky, waste	
Veronica agrestis	Green Field-speedwell	A	up to 10 cm	Mar–Nov	All soils	
Veronica alpina	Alpine Speedwell	P	up to 30 cm	Jul–Aug	Damp, rocky, mountains, meadows	
Veronica anagallis-aquatica	Blue Water-Speedwell	P	up to 60 cm	Jun–Aug	Wet, muddy, river, pond, stream and lake margins	99
Veronica arvensis	Wall Speedwell	A	up to 30 cm	Mar–Oct	Dry, grassy, heaths, walls	
Veronica beccabunga	Brooklime	P	up to 60 cm	May–Sep	Ditches, pond, river and lake margins	99
Veronica catenata	Pink Water-Speedwell	P	up to 60 cm	Jun–Aug	Slow-moving water, rivers, ponds, streams	
Veronica chamaedrys	Germander Speedwell	P	up to 30 cm	Mar–Jul	Grassy, banks, waste, woods	
Veronica fruticans	Rock Speedwell	P	up to 30 cm	Jul–Sep	Grassy, rocky, mountains	
Veronica hederifolia	Ivy-leaved Speedwell	A	up to 10 cm	Mar–Aug	All soils	
Veronica montana	Wood Speedwell	P	up to 30 cm	Apr–Jul	Damp woods	
Veronica officinalis	Heath Speedwell	P	up to 30 cm	May–Aug	Dry, grassy, heaths, woods	
Veronica polita	Grey Field-speedwell	A	up to 10 cm	Jan–Dec	Cultivated land	
Veronica scutellata	Marsh Speedwell	P	up to 60 cm	Jun–Aug	Wet, acid, marshes, bogs, meadows, ditches	
Veronica serpyllifolia	Thyme-leaved Speedwell	P	up to 10 cm	Mar–Oct	Grassy, waste, cultivated land	
Veronica spicata	Spiked Speedwell	P	up to 60 cm	Jul–Oct	Dry, chalky, grassy, rocky, woods	
Veronica triphyllos	Fingered Speedwell	A	up to 30 cm	Apr–Jul	Light sandy soils, waste, arable, cultivated land	
Veronica verna	Spring Speedwell	A	up to 30 cm	May–Jul	Dry, grassy, pastures	
Viburnum lantana	Wayfaring-tree	T	up to 6 m	Apr–Jun	Chalky, scrub, woods	
Viburnum opulus	Guelder-rose	P	up to 4 m	Jun–Jul	Wet, woods, hedgerows	
Vicia bithynica	Bithynian Vetch	A	up to 60 cm	May–Jun	Coastal, grassy, scrub, cliffs	
Vicia cracca	Tufted Vetch	P	up to 2 m	Jun–Aug	Grassy, meadows, scrub, banks, coastal shingle	
Vicia hirsuta	Hairy Tare	A	up to 60 cm	May–Aug	Dry, grassy, woods, scrub, cult. land	
Vicia lathyroides	Spring Vetch	A	up to 30 cm	May–Jun	Grassy, arable, heaths, waste	
Vicia lutea	Yellow-vetch	A	up to 10 cm	Jun–Sep	Coastal, shingle, sandy, cliffs, rough grassy	
Vicia orobus	Wood Bitter-vetch	P	up to 60 cm	May–Jun	Rough grass, cliffs	
Vicia parviflora	Slender Tare	A	up to 60 cm	Jun–Aug	Grassy, scrub, hedges, banks	
Vicia sativa	Common Vetch	A	up to 90 cm	Apr–Sep	Grassy, meadows, hedges, road verges, cultivated land	
Vicia sepium	Bush Vetch	P	up to 90 cm	May–Nov	Chalky, slightly acid, grassy, scrub, hedges	
Vicia sylvatica	Wood Vetch	P	up to 2 m	Jun–Aug	Rocky, scrub, woods, coastal cliffs	
Vicia tetrasperma	Smooth Tare	A	up to 60 cm	May–Aug	Grassy, chalky, scrub, road verges	
Viola arvensis	Field Pansy	A	up to 30 cm	Apr–Oct	Chalky, neutral soils, waste, arable	
Viola canina	Heath Dog-violet	P	up to 30 cm	Apr–Jul	Grassy, woods, heaths, fens, dunes	
Viola hirta	Hairy Violet	P	up to 10 cm	Mar–Jun	Chalky, grassy, woods, scrub	101
Viola kitaibeliana	Dwarf Pansy	A	up to 10 cm	Mar–Jul	Dry, sandy, arable	
Viola lactea	Pale Dog-violet	P	up to 30 cm	May–Jun	Dry, acid, heaths	
Viola lutea	Mountain Pansy	P	up to 30 cm	Apr–Jul	Grassy, rocky, acid, chalky	
Viola odorata	Sweet Violet	P	up to 10 cm	Feb–May	Chalky, neutral, woods, ledges, scrub	
Viola palustris	Marsh Violet	P	up to 10 cm	Apr–Jul	Wet, marshes, heaths, woods, acid heaths	101
Viola persicifolia	Fen Violet	P	up to 30 cm	May–Jun	Marshes, fens	
Viola reichenbachiana	Early Dog-violet	P	up to 10 cm	Mar–Jun	Shady, woods, ledges	101
Viola riviniana	Common Dog-violet	P	up to 30 cm	Apr–Jun	Grassy, woods, heaths, downs	
Viola rupestris	Teesdale Violet	P	up to 10 cm	Mar–Jul	Dry, limestone, gravel, heaths, meadows	
Viola tricolor	Wild Pansy	A/P	up to 30 cm	Apr–Oct	Grassy, waste, arable, cultivated land	101
Viscum album	Mistletoe	P	up to 60 cm	Feb–Apr	Parasitic, decid. woods	
Vulpia bromoides	Squirreltail Fescue	A	up to 60 cm	May–Jul	Dry, bare ground, waste	
Vulpia ciliata	Bearded Fescue	A	up to 60 cm	May–Jul	Coastal, shingle, sandy	
Vulpia fasciculata	Dune Fescue	A	up to 60 cm	May–Jul	Grassy, coastal, sand dunes	
Vulpia myuros	Rat's-tail Fescue	A	up to 60 cm	May–Jul	Dry, bare ground	
Vulpia unilateralis	Mat-grass Fescue	A	up to 20 cm	May–Jul	Chalky, grassy	
Wahlenbergia hederacea	Ivy-leaved Bellflower	P	up to 10 cm	Jul–Aug	Peaty, acid soils	
Wolffia arrhiza	Rootless Duckweed	P	up to 1 mm	Jun–Jul	Aquatic, floating	
Woodsia alpina	Alpine Woodsia	P	up to 6 cm	Jun–Aug	Basic rocks, mountains	
Woodsia ilvensis	Oblong Woodsia	P	up to 20 cm	Jul–Sep	Rocks, mountains	
Zannichellia palustris	Horned Pondweed	P	up to 50 cm	May–Aug	Aquatic, submerged, freshwater ponds	
Zostera angustifolia	Narrow-leaved Eelgrass	P	up to 30 cm	Jun–Sep	Submerged, marine, estuaries	
Zostera marina	Eelgrass	P	up to 60 cm	Jun–Sep	Submerged, marine, sandy, gravel, shores	
Zostera noltei	Dwarf Eelgrass	P	up to 12 cm	Jun–Oct	Submerged, marine, estuaries, backwaters	

Suppliers and Addresses

Ashton Wold Wildflowers
Ashton Wold, Peterborough PE8 5LZ
T 01832 273 575 / 020 7435 0803

Boston Seeds
47 Spilsby Road, Boston, Lincolnshire
T 01205 358 864
E awallis@bostonseeds.co.uk
www.bostonseeds.co.uk

British Flora (Glyn Onione)
Grange Farm Nursery, Grange Road,
Widmer End, High Wycombe
Buckinghamshire HP15 6AE
T 01494 718 203
E glyn@britishflora.co.uk
www.britishflora.co.uk

British Seed Houses Ltd
Bewsey Industrial Estate
Pitt Street, Warrington WA5 5LE
T 01925 654 411
F 01925 230 682
Email: seeds@bshwarr.co.uk

British Wild Flower Plants
(Linda Laxton)
31 Main Road, North Burlingham,
Norwich, Norfolk NR13 4TA
T&F 01603 716 615
E linda@wildflowers.co.uk
www.wildflowers.co.uk

Burntwood Nurseries
The Estate Office, Burntwood,
Winchester, Hampshire SO21 1AF
T 01962 881 514
F 01962 886 788

Clara Slater Plants
Archenhills, Stanford Bishop,
Bringsty, Worcestershire WR6 5TZ
T 01886 884 721

Conservation Volunteers Northern Ireland
Beech House, 159 Raven Hill Road,
Belfast BT6 0BP
T 028 9064 5169
F 028 9064 4409
E e.bann@cvni.org
www.cvni.org

Cumbria Wildflowers (Openspace)
37 Norfolk Road, Carlisle,
Cumbria CA2 5PQ
T&F 01228 402 182
E Openspace@breathe.com
www.openspace.gb.com

Design by Nature
Monavea Cross, Crettyard, Carlow, Eire
T 056 42526
F 056 42722
E info@allgowild.com
www.allgowild.com

DLF (trifolium) Ltd
Inkberrow, Worcestershire WR7 4LJ
T 01386 791 102
F 01385 792 715
E amenity@dlf.co.uk
www.perryfields.co.uk

Eco Seeds Ltd
1 Bar View Cottages, Shore Road,
Strangford, County Down BT30 7NN
T 02844 881 227
E eco-seeds@strangford.fsnet.co.uk

H. Edmunds
Estate Office, Cholderton, Salisbury,
Wiltshire SP4 0DR
T 01980 629 203
F 01980 629 307

Emorsgate Seeds (Richard Brown)
Limes Farm, Tilney All Saints,
King's Lynn, Norfolk PE34 4RT
T 01553 829 028
F 01553 829 803
www.wildseed.co.uk

The English Wildflower Company
(Gayle and John Schumacher)
The Lakes, Yew Tree Lane, Rotherfield,
East Sussex TN6 3QP
T 01892 661 755
www.englishwildflowers.com

Flower Farms
Carvers Hill Farm, Shalbourne,
Marlborough, Wiltshire SN8 3PS
T&F 01672 870 782
E flower.farms@farmersweekly.net
www.wildflowerfarms.com

Forestart Ltd
Church Farm, Hadnall, Shrewsbury,
Shropshire SY4 4AQ
T 01939 210638
F 01939 210563
Email: info@forestart.co.uk
www.forestart.co.uk

Hardy Orchids
New Gate Farm, Scotchey Lane, Stour
Provost, Gillingham, Dorset SP8 5LT
T 01747 838368
F 01747 838308
E Hardyorchids@supanet.com
www.hardyorchids.supanet.com

Heritage Seeds
Osmington, Weymouth,
Dorset DT3 6EX
T 01305 834 504
F 01305 835 911
E mail@hseeds.fsnet.co.uk
www.heritageseeds.co.uk

Hurrel & McLean Seeds
(Nick Gladstone), South Hall Farm,
Beverley Road, Cranswick, Driffield,
East Yorkshire YO25 9PF
T 01377 271 400/500
E Nick@hurrellandmclean.
freeserve.co.uk

John Robinthwaite
14 Burdett Road, Stonehouse,
Gloucestershire GL10 2JW
T&F 01453 821 246
E limwetplants@hotmail.com

Johanna Westgate
Brambles, Laburnum Terrace,
Abbotskerswell, Newton Abbott,
South Devon TQ12 5PT
T 01626 364 652
E johanna_westgate@hotmail.com

John Shipton
Y Felin, Henllan Amgoed, Whitland,
Carmarthenshire SA34 0DL
T 01994 240 125
F 01994 241 180
E bluebell@zoo.co.uk

Landlife
National Wildflower Centre,
Court Hey Park, Liverpool L16 3NA
T 0151 737 1819
F 0151 737 1820
E info@landlife.org.uk
www.landlife.org.uk /
www.nwc.org.uk

Merton Hall Pond Ltd
Merton Estate Office, Merton,
Thetford, Norfolk IP25 6QH
T 01953 881 763
F 01953 884 020

Mike Handyside (wild flowers)
15 The Old Paddock, Main Road,
Goostrey, Crewe, Cheshire CW4 8QZ
T&F 01477 549 336

Mike Mullis (wildflower plants)
1 Chantry Cottages, Warbleton,
Heathfield, East Sussex TN21 9PT
T 01435 830 578
E mm.wfp@mullis27.fsnet.co.uk

Mires Beck Nursery
Low Mill Lane, North Cave, Brough,
East Yorkshire HU15 2NR
T&F 01430 421 543
E Admin@miresbeck.co.uk
www.miresbeck.co.uk

Natural Selection
1 Station Cottages, Hullavington,
Chippenham, Wiltshire SN14 6ET
T 01666 837 369
E martin@worldmutation
www.worldmutation.demon.co.uk

Natural Surroundings
Bayfield Estate, Holt, Norfolk NR25 7JN
T 01263 711 091
E loosley@farmersweekly.net

North Somerset Natives
c/o Ellen McDoual, 65 Walton Road,
Clevedon BS21 6AR
T 01275 875 485

Northumberland Wildflowers
Hunter's Hollow, Todstead,
Longframlington, Northumberland
NE65 8AU
T 01665 570 207
www.northumberlandwildflowers.co.uk

Open Space (Cumbria) Ltd
Jonathon Rook, 37 Norfolk Road,
Carlisle, Cumbria CA2 5PQ
T&F 01228 402 182
E openspace@breathe.com

Poyntzfield Herb Nursery (Garve
Scott-Lodge), Black Isle, Dingwall,
Ross-shire IV7 8LX
T 01381 610 352
E info@poyntzfieldherbs.co.uk
www.poyntzfieldherbs.co.uk

**Really Wild Flowers/
HV Horticulture Ltd**
Spring Mead, Bedchester, Shaftsbury,
Dorset SP7 0JU
T 01747 811 778
F 01747 811 499
E RWFlowers@aol.com
www.reallywildflowers.co.uk

Scotia Seeds (Giles Laverack)
Mavisbank, Farnell
Brechin
Angus DD9 6TR
Tel: 01356 626 425
Fax: 01356 629 183
Email: scotiaseeds@btconnect.com
www.scotiaseeds.co.uk

Scottish Origins LLP
3 Brewery Lane, Kinross KY13 8EL
T 01577 861437
E info@scotorigins.co.uk
www.scotorigins.co.uk

Scott's Wildflowers
Swallow Hill Barn, 31 Common Side,
Distington, Workington
T 01946 830 486
E wildflowers@btinternet.com
www.scottswildflowers.co.uk

Sue Everett
122 Derwent Road, Thatcham,
Berkshire
T 01635 847 164
E suejeverett@hotmail.com

TGS Wildflowers
1 Kings Road, Evesham,
Worcs WR11 3BP
T 01386 45868
E tony@gardeningwild.co.uk

Weald Meadows Initiative
High Weald AONB Unit
Woodland Enterprise Centre
Flimwell, East Sussex TN5 7PR
T 01580 879 500
F 01580 879 499
E meadows@highweald.org
www.highweald.org

West Coast Gardens
Dorminack, St Buryan, Penzance,
Cornwall TR19 6BH
T 01736 810 087

Wild Plant Services
Dean Hall Farm, Littlebeck Lane,
Sneaton, Whitby, North Yorkshire
YO22 5HY
E Wildplant@onetel.net.uk

Wiltshire Wildflower Seed
T&F 01380 848 132
E andrewmacdonald@
specialitycrops.co.uk

Yarningdale Nurseries Ltd
16 Chapel Street, Warwick CV34 4HL
T 01926 842 282
F 01926 842 404

Yellow Flag Wildflowers
8 Plock Court, Longford,
Gloucestershire GL2 9DW
T&F 01452 311 525
E enquiries@wildflowers
www.wildflowersuk.com

Index

Page numbers in *italic* refer to the illustrations

Acknowledgements

I would gratefully like to thank the
following for all their patient help and
advice, but especially English Nature
and Di Gent, without whose help
I would still be trying to complete
this book.

Steve Berry of English Nature, Lewes,
Sussex, for giving so much invaluable
advice, being instrumental in
obtaining permission to reproduce
many of the images from English
Nature's picture library in
Northampton, scrutinizing and
reading the proofs, and much more.

English Nature, Northampton, for
access to their picture library and for
allowing some of their images to be
reproduced – the use of which has
been invaluable to this book.

Di Gent of Crowthorne, Berkshire,
who annotated the complete list of
British native plants that appears at
the back of the book.

Rob Hume, Editor, RSPB Magazine,
for use of the quote by the late Roger
Fitter in the introduction.

Donald McIntyre of Manor Farm,
Langridge, Bath, who took me round
his meadows and gave much useful
advice.

Bruce Middleton of Down Close,
Heyshott, West Sussex, who kindly
took me round many habitats and
waited patiently whilst I
photographed many rare and unusual
wild plants.

Mike Mullis of Warbleton, Heathfield,
East Sussex, for his contribution to
the section on growing orchids,
allowing me to 'rifle' through his
collection of wild plants, for kindly
reading the proofs and much more.

Sussex Biodiversity Centre for kindly
supplying the locations of many wild
plants.

Also thanks to those who took me
round their 'wild' gardens, and to the
many who put up with my endless
phone calls. Also to Doreen and Polly
who patiently accompanied me on
some of my wild flower-hunting trips.